Praise for *7 Mindsets to*

"If you are ready to gain a deeper understanding as to specific mindsets that will allow you to experience a more rewarding and deeply fulfilled life, you will benefit from the wisdom contained within this book!"

~Jill Lublin, International Speaker & Best Selling Author of *Get Noticed, Get Referrals; Guerrilla Publicity;* and *Networking Magic;* JillLublin.com

"7 Mindsets to Master Self Awareness is a fresh and unique masterpiece that clearly outlines the connection between what is happening in our chakras with what is happening in our subconscious. With in depth and easy to understand explanations, Elizabeth Diamond effortlessly empowers you with essential knowledge and practical exercises you need to power up your chakras and mind to create the life of balance, love and fulfillment you have been craving for. 5 stars all the way!"

~Cindy Ashton, Performer, Speaker, Author & Expert in Overcoming Obstacles

"Elizabeth has an extraordinarily positive and powerful message and a captivating, unique approach to awakening you to what is possible in your life. Integrate these "*7 Mindsets*" into your way of life, realize your potential and step into a place of fulfillment. Read the profound wisdom and feel the pure joy in these pages!"

~Marilyn Gordon, Life Transformation Teacher, Hypnotherapist, and Author of *The Wise Mind.*

Liz has brilliantly revealed the inner truth, purpose and meaning of life of the individual in this most amazing book. She has combined many ancient teachings with a modern understanding to create a most magnificent and easy to follow process of transformation. "7 Mindsets" is a life changing read! If you're looking for ways to tap into your authentic self and live life as intended...this is the book for you!

~Jamie Jones, Tao Jones Exchange and Author of *You Are Amazing!*

7 MINDSETS

to Master Self-Awareness

ELIZABETH DIAMOND

authorHOUSE®

AuthorHouse™
1663 Liberty Drive
Bloomington, IN 47403
www.authorhouse.com
Phone: 1-800-839-8640

First published by AuthorHouse 7/9/2010

ISBN: 978-1-4520-4625-9 (e)
ISBN: 978-1-4520-4623-5 (sc)
ISBN: 978-1-4520-4624-2 (hc)

Library of Congress Control Number: 2010910137

Printed in the United States of America
Bloomington, Indiana

This book is printed on acid-free paper.

This book is dedicated to the divine force present in all things that constantly pushes me to grow, expand and become more of who I already am.

And to my Great Uncle, Waldemar J. Kaminski, a promise made long ago is now fulfilled.

You are invited to join our interactive
community for mastering self-awareness…
TODAY!!!!

www.masterselfawareness.com

CONTENTS

PREFACE

We currently live during a time where many different avenues hold the possibility of leading a person towards the realization of their deepest truths. No matter what path is chosen, there is a single common factor that plays a role every time, the activation of self-awareness. When a person is able to shine the light of their awareness into every moment of their life, no matter what is happening, true mastery of the self is reached.

The solid foundation that self-awareness creates is so strong that it is capable of sustaining ever increasing states of positive well-being to fill every arena of life. The journey of awareness is to discover the essence of one's authentic self. Once a person is able to grasp the core of who they really are, their true divine nature, they can allow that knowing to empower them to make vital evolutionary leaps.

On my path to self-awareness, I have discovered that all that is required to get started is a willingness to show up and explore what is possible in your life. After making personal transformational shifts and through the observation of the profound changes taking place in my clients lives, I have concluded that there is nothing more significant than for one to arrive at the decision to finally surrender the need to struggle and at the same time summon the courage and desire to awaken the knowing of their fullest potential. Change originates first on the inside. It begins with changing how you think so that you can initiate the process of feeling better, right now in this very moment. When you feel great on the inside, miracles start to unfold in your life.

Before you actively explore the 7 Mindsets revealed in this book, take a few minutes right now to check in with yourself. Notice how your body is feeling, notice how you feel emotionally, notice what types of thoughts are running through your mind. When you are ready, close your eyes and imagine what your life would look and feel like to:

- reach a state of unshakeable peace, one that remains steady and does not fluctuate.
- finally achieve freedom from worry, struggle, lack, limitation, and fear.
- completely relax into the flow of your life.
- surrender to a natural organic unfolding of events.
- enjoy the process of discovering the strengths and talents that make you unique.
- be conscious of a vital sense of aliveness present at the core of your soul.
- maintain a focused awareness of every moment by remaining present with yourself.

When you are finished performing this exercise, take a moment to scan your body once again and notice how different you feel. Do you feel more relaxed? Is your mood lighter? Are you enjoying a stream of thought that is more pleasant in nature? The way of life described above is possible when you become aware of what you choose to focus upon in your life. The 7 Mindsets outlined in this book are designed to guide you to cultivate a foundation of awareness that allows you to infuse the radiant light of your true authentic self into every single one of your daily actions from the ordinary to the extraordinary.

No matter where you are in the journey of your life, you always hold within you the potential to realize the highest version of you. The key to achieving a deeply fulfilling and rewarding lifestyle is to discover ways that incline you to feel good now. When you make it your dominant intent to think good feeling thoughts, to live as though you already have all the things that you desire, and take inspired action from an internal starting point that feels whole and complete, the experiences in your external surrounding begin to change to reflect what is being felt on the internal realms.

Your life is happening right now. How you feel in this moment determines whether or not you are truly living the life you really want. When you feel good it means that you are allowing all the things that you really desire to flow into your life experience, if you feel frustrated, sad or unhappy it means that there are blocks in place preventing you from reaching the lifestyle that you deserve to live.

Your current state of being, your consciousness, is represented by an overall feeling that is produced within the body as a result of all thought and action put forth up until this moment. The nature of a person's consciousness is a choice, a way of approaching and viewing life. If you are not satisfied with the life you are living then it is up to you to make the decision to change your perspective. It starts with becoming aware of what you are thinking and feeling in every moment and realizing your ability to choose new ways of viewing the world in order to begin feeling good now. To experience lasting and sustainable change in life, one must initiate the process of transforming from the inside out. When you commit to the practice of observing how you think and feel about your life, you create the opportunity to embrace a new way of being in this world.

Determining which thoughts allow you to experience the optimal well-being that is reflective of your natural divine state is to find ways that allow you to tune into the eternal wisdom already present within you. Because we feel so physical and experience the mind as the center of the universe, our true essence, our natural state of being becomes lost or forgotten over time. The process of returning to the remembrance of who we really are at the core of our soul is to spend time and energy seeking out our bliss, our deepest passions, the things, the activities, or events that arouse profound states of joy. This opens the door for our inner light to shine forth. It is when our heart, body and mind become filled with the light of knowing our true purpose in life that we are able to finally step into our brilliance and unleash its magnificence.

It is our purpose is to feel ever expanding amounts of joy and well-being, and enjoy the natural unfolding of events taking place in our life. If we are struggling in adversity, feeling frustrated or always wanting something better, then it is vital to commit to the discovery of new ways that allow us to feel better straight away so that we can soon begin to realize our true purpose. In order to move from where you are to where you want to be, a person must be willing to go within, to explore the depths of their being and tune into how they feel on the inside. The moment we place our focused awareness on how we feel internally, a space opens for something new to be created.

Therefore, to initiate the process of perceiving the world from a place that is grounded in divine truth, it is crucial to spend time each day coming to know what our natural state of being looks and feels like. Who we are at the core is pure feeling, a sensation that cannot be described by words or fully understood by the thoughts of the mind. The best way to tune into our soul's true presence is to clear the mind and relax deeply into the body. Once we become familiar with the sensation of our natural state of being, we can intentionally call forth its quality to permeate our awareness.

As human beings, we possess an inherent ability to harness the creative power of our thoughts to increase our capacity to feel good. The more we entertain new and radically different thought patterns and arouse specific feelings to support them we enable ourselves to become familiar with the new sensation being held within the body. This automatically increases our set points to allow increased amounts of positive energy to flow into every experience of our lives. The great news is that because we have already spent time feeling into the essence of our desired experiences, when they do begin to manifest at the external level, we are able to sustain the positive flow of events without having to worry about unconsciously sabotaging them. The more we endure a prolonged focused awareness on desired patterns of thinking and feeling, the easier they become to sustain. Before you know it, they become a way of life. We literally embody them over time. Once the new pattern dominates our way of being, it ultimately plays a larger role by attracting the physical equivalent of what is being felt on the internal realms to be manifested into our life experiences.

The path of self-awareness is a journey that is always growing and expanding. It truly is a process of becoming where you hold the potential to infinitely ascend on an upward spiral of positive emotional experiences. Your life can be as wonderful and magnificent as you allow it to be. As human beings, we are constantly being called to live a rewarding and meaningful life. The secret is to allow happiness to flow into everything you do. Being happy in every moment enables you to profoundly experience the joy and peace that is your natural state of being. Travel in the direction of deliberately choosing thoughts that feel good and you will be filled with the essence of that which you are searching for.

This book is intended to assist you in calling forth good feeling aspects of yourself in which you can immerse your thoughts. As always, it is important to take the time to ponder the insight of each mindset and apply the exercises into your daily actions. Success is yours when you begin to implement the new words, thoughts and feelings being presented into your life. You will discover a shift in your consciousness that awakens you to a deeper awareness of the infinite possibilities of your soul.

Now is the time to let go of all you thought you were and move into a new level of understanding of who you really are. Connect with your unlimited potential and allow infinite wisdom, joy, love and well-being to flow into every area of your life. You are worth it!

Here's to enjoying the journey of your life!

May all your intentions be fulfilled!

Elizabeth Diamond

ACKNOWLEDGEMENTS

I would like to express my deepest appreciation to every single member of my family. Each person has offered their love and support over the years in their own unique way. Those kind acts are recognized and have profoundly imprinted my heart and soul for eternity.

I am so grateful to have met in the early years of my adulthood, my first spiritual teacher, Marilyn Gordon, whose radiant light sparked within me an awakening to the awareness of my divine potential and a powerful desire to fully remember who I am. Thank you for your generous gifts of transformational knowledge, profound wisdom and loving support.

I would like to acknowledge the loving support of one of my greatest mentors, Sydney Ryba. All of the knowledge and guidance that you so generously shared with me continues to awaken me to a deeper understanding of my divine purpose.

I am in awe of my manger and publicist, Jennifer Geronimo, whose unbridled enthusiasm for my work and her unerring belief in me continue to inspire me on a daily basis. Your support keeps me moving forward and has been invaluable to me especially during times of intense change. For that, I am deeply moved in which there are no words to fully express it. My heartfelt appreciation and love go out to you. I am blessed to have you in my life.

To my loyal and loving soul sisters, Nancie Irwin and her mother, Rosemary Hughes, who are two of the most phenomenal and courageous women I have had the privilege of sharing time and energy with.

To Inriel Romero, the best project manager and product launch developer ever!!! Your encouragement and innovative ideas sparked new inspiration within me allowing all of my projects to grow and expand in massive ways! Thank you for your loyal efforts and for showing up as a soul friend!

To Yaan Gulledge whose strong sense of integrity and noble presence graced my life in many, many unseen ways. Thanks for being an angel in my life and my affiliate manager!

To my wonderful, supportive and gracious neighbors, Jill & Jeff Berdysiak, Paula Carroll, Amber (from across the street) who kept an ever watchful eye on my girls as they ran around the neighborhood and providing me the space I needed to retreat into my writing cave so that I could complete this book and share it with the world!

To Fahmi Basaleh for all of your brilliant graphic designs for the cover and interior of this book, working with you was truly effortless!

To Lydia Maybee for thinking outside of the box and really seeing me for who I truly am during our portrait session. I am blessed to have had a glimpse into your passion!

And my heartfelt thanks goes out to all the wonderful souls who believe in me, supported me in unseen ways as I wrote this book, and encouraged me to become the person I am today: Jamie Jones, Jill Lublin, Kim Markison Duyette, Elvia Perez, Rebecca Sheldon, Isabelle Choiniere, Beth Barany, Cheryl Liqouri, Kristi One Feather, Andrew Luce, Daniela Costa, and Sheri Ashton.

My love goes out to every single one of my friends and clients who have enhanced the quality of my life over the years. You know who you are!

INTRODUCTION

"There is more wisdom in your body than in your
deepest philosophy." – Friedrich Nietzsche

There is deeper meaning to the phrases "being conscious" and "being unconscious" than you may realize. If you asked me to describe the difference between "being conscious" and "being unconscious" when I was in my early twenties, I would have thought you were referring to medical terms. Either I was physically alert and awake, conscious, or I was unconscious, knocked out cold or asleep. Although many people are waking up to the awareness of what it means to live consciously, it is my intent to shed some light on its deeper and more profound meaning.

I recently listened to a radio talk show as the host expressed what she felt was the extreme liberal and over use of the word conscious. She was making a statement about a conversation she recently entertained on the subject of conscious decision making. She emphatically stated, "Of course I am conscious when I make decisions, how can I possibly make a decision when I am asleep and unconscious?" After hearing that remark, I realized that the content contained within this book has the potential to clarify what it means to live with conscious self-awareness while offering simple guidance that can assist your journey of personal discovery to realizing just how powerful and brilliant you already are.

Because there is such wide usage of these two terms today with a variety of interpretations, I decided to take the opportunity to remind you of its ancient context, one that appears to have been lost over the ages. In reminding you of its hidden meaning, as to how one lives with conscious awareness, it is my hope that you will gain deeper insight into the true nature of your existence.

The mainstream definition of the word conscious describes one who is alert, awake and aware of their internal and external surroundings. Although this is its most familiar designation, the depth of its ancient context far surpasses our modern day connotation. Ancient civilizations along with many philosophers over the ages have viewed consciousness as the most important thing in this universe. They were aware of the notion that each individual is filled with the presence of the infinite divine source that flows through all things in this universe and is accessible to each and every one of us in all moments. Understanding that they could harness and direct this creative intelligence, they applied it according to their unique talents and wrote about it for centuries.

What exactly does this mean to our modern day society? How can we apply this knowledge to achieve personal awareness? The answer, the "secret", lies in one's ability to release their illusion of self-identification with external resources to embrace the eternal truth of the soul. It is a scientifically proven fact that we are more than just a physical body. When one explores all matter in this world at an atomic level, we discover that everything is varying rates of vibrating energy. All matter is different configurations of atomic and molecular combinations. As energy manifests itself into physical form, it reflects different degrees of light and color. Although our bodies appear to be physical in form, at the basic level of our existence, we are nothing more than vibrating energy that is condensing to ultimately manifest a form of matter that we refer to as our physical body. Thoughts and emotions are nothing more than varying frequencies of vibrating energy as well. It is the infinite intelligence within our consciousness that guides our body to materialize into physical shape and form and will continue to sustain it until death. If it were not for our consciousness, our physical body would cease to exist. We are not bodies possessing a consciousness, we are consciousness manifesting a body and at the same time our subsequent physical experiences.

When we explore the human body at a cellular level, we have determined that every single cell is an individual consciousness that works together to support the whole. Each cell is intelligent and contains memory. Our cells record and store every single event that has happened to us since the time of birth. Science has yet to explain where the intelligence of cells originates from. In fact, science will never be able to explain the inner workings of consciousness because it is a direct manifestation of the infinite creative intelligence which is non-physical and unlimited in its scope.

To fully comprehend the truth of one's existence is to explore the inner realms of one's consciousness. It is when one takes the time to explore the depths of the soul that they can begin to touch upon a deeper understanding of the divine infinite source that is greater than the self. The creative intelligence that flows through each and every thing in this universe is filled with endless possibility. Every person has the same potential in their individual development to direct energy to manifest according to desired outcomes. Becoming aware of this inner reality, the truth of one's being, a person begins to awaken to the awareness of the potential of creative thought. As humans we create with every thought. Every single thought we entertain has a creative effect on the body. Each thought either strengthens us or weakens us.

Our bodies react to whatever our mind is processing and interpreting. Every single thought triggers a neurological response in the brain which then produces equivalent physiological and emotional responses in the body. Chemical reactions are released from our organs in response to our thoughts. Our thoughts guide and direct the physical well-being of the body. We can determine through the experience of our emotions whether or not our thoughts are directing our bodies to wholeness and well-being. Life affirming thoughts support all the processes of the body. Thoughts that are not life affirming trigger the release of stress chemistry which slowly breaks down all systems of the body over time producing experiences of dis-ease at every level. Positive emotional experiences are a direct result of positive thinking and negative emotional experiences are a result of negative thoughts.

The great news is that you are in control of your thoughts. Your power lies in the way you choose to create with your thoughts. You are a creative being with an unlimited amount of potential. What you choose to place your attention and focus on is what you will attract into your life. It is up to you to decide to channel the creative force of your thought to manifest experiences that you truly desire. Achieving happiness, perfect health, abundance, well-being and anything else you can imagine is a decision to be made according to your unique preferences. Once you choose it, you can direct the mind to achieve it through a constant stream of focused attention.

It is the intent of this book is to assist you in the awakening to the awareness of your consciousness. By using the word conscious, I mean that you will become more aware of the creative effect of every thought on your physical existence. You have the power to design a destiny that is shaped to your unique talents and passions in life. The process of self- awareness is an empowering journey. It is a continuous process of expanding and becoming more. You can achieve a lasting happiness, inner peace and well-being that is not dependent of mere chance and circumstance but rather the direct result of your conscious intent. Creating authentic states of sustainable joy and freedom is within your reach in this very moment. The key is to keep your awareness and attention on what feels best and really matters to you.

There are seven different mindsets outlined in this book. The intention of each mindset is to activate its corresponding energy center in the body otherwise known as a chakra. Each chapter contains insight into the nature of the mindset being awakened, positive affirmations, and a recommended crystal with a description of how it can support and enhance the process of self-discovery. As you place your focused attention on mastering each mindset, you will open to a greater sense of personal awareness. The entire progression guides you to move into alignment with your personal source of inner wisdom. Once connected, you will gain access to a deeper understanding of the infinite essence of the divine intelligence that flows through you and serves to create and hold the entire whole of this universe.

Our energy body contains seven major chakras, which means "wheel" or "disk" in Sanskrit. The Chakra System is an ancient Indian concept that is now a legitimate holistic model for health and wellness recognized by western medical practitioners. The chakras are located along the spine spaced in intervals from the tailbone to the crown of the head. They are depicted as spinning vortexes of energy that look like lotus flowers. While they are located within the energy body, they connect, interconnect and directly affect the physical, mental and emotional bodies, thus reinforcing the truth that one cannot separate the effects of thought and emotion from the body.

Chakras absorb and project energy in the form of color and light. When the chakras are opened, they are clear and balanced and one is able to experience a harmony that is the truth of their being. If the chakras are closed, that means that they are blocked and imbalanced, and one experiences disharmony or discord within their body. Each chakra has a unique frequency of vibration and responds to color, light, smell, and sound in different ways. Although each chakra possesses its own unique wisdom, they all connect to and interpenetrate one another to allow the flow of spirit. For a person to experience perfect balance and wholeness, all the chakras must be opened in order to attune to the divine perfection of the universe.

Since color and light have profound effects on the energy systems of the body and one's emotions, a crystal is recommended along with its unique properties to assist in the mastering of each specific mindset. Crystals are powerful tools in balancing and effecting change on subtle levels. The way in which the atoms and molecules arrange themselves in perfect unity make crystals the most stable and balanced form of matter on the planet. Because of their perfected form, crystals produce high energetic frequencies. Their brilliant colors and radiant amounts of light automatically bring the chakras into balance. They instantly remove blockages by restoring light and renewing energy. Because crystals are naturally attuned to the divine perfection of the universe, they easily surface the wisdom inherent in each chakra. They also amplify the energy of our thoughts, intentions and visualizations. The last chapter of this book will explain how to successfully activate and program a crystal to assist you in accessing the truth of your being through intention setting and creative processes.

We are pure forms of manifested consciousness. Our outer experiences are a reflection of our inner state of mind. This is the truth of our being. The awareness of our free will ability to choose and decide the nature of our thoughts in every moment leads to the development of self-awareness, and self-awareness is consciousness realizing itself. Allow that which is eternal in you to rise up and guide you to embrace the joy and freedom that is your divine inheritance.

～

"This BEing human is a guest house.
Every morning a new arrival.
A joy, a depression, a meanness,
some momentary awareness comes
as an unexpected visitor.
Welcome and entertain all!
Even if they're a crowd of sorrows,
who violently sweep your house
empty of its furniture,
still, treat each guest honorably.
He may be clearing you out
for some new delight.
The dark thought, the shame, the malice,
meet them at the door laughing,
and invite them in.
Be grateful for whomever comes,
because each has been sent
as a guide from beyond."
- Rumi

～

Moving Through the Chakra System

1

"There is deep wisdom within our very flesh, if we can only come to our senses and feel it." ~ Elizabeth A. Behnke

Moving Through The Chakra System

The chakra system is where our reality holds the potential to form and transform. Each center possesses a unique rate of vibration that moves up in frequency as one ascends from the root to the crown. Different aspects of being are represented in the individual centers. The root chakra holds the slowest frequencies and the crown the highest. By tuning into the emotional sensations that each mindset produces in the body, the deeper wisdom inherent in each chakras is called forth to unfold and blossom into our awareness. When new insight is gained, a gate opens for one to move into the elevated frequencies of the next chakra. Continuing on the upward spiral of higher vibrations to feeling better, a person moves closer to realizing their true authentic nature. The journey of mastering self- awareness allows one to shed attachment to and identification with their mind and their physical form. Upon reaching the crown, a person experiences the oneness and totality that is their natural state of being. The true self is realized. Sitting in the presence of who you really are strengthens ones awareness of the depth of their creative potential, their divinity, and their connection to the whole.

The seven different mindsets are a guide for shifting one's awareness to fully embrace the many wonderful and positive aspects of being vitally alive. Placing the principles of these mindsets into action forges a direct pathway to the source of all possibility. Once this connection is established, it enables one to draw unlimited amounts of inspiration from its infinite supply on a moment to moment basis. Not only will you begin to relax into a profound sense of inner fulfillment, uniting with the divine source awakens one to a constant presence of intuitive knowing. In order to successfully integrate and embody the divine inspiration accessed at the crown, the information must be intentionally channeled back down the passageway of the chakras for manifestation into physical form. A return journey to the root is necessary in order to infuse the light of divine inspiration into every single one of our daily interactions from the most mundane to the most remarkable and exceptional of experiences.

The more time spent feeling into and exploring each one of the *7 Mindsets* only serves to fortify one's ability to remain aware of the existing presence of their natural state of being. As this connection is nourished, so is our capacity to manifest the awareness of it into our physical actions. Each time we move through this process, we become more deeply rooted in the highest wisdom discovered at the crown. We literally become anchored into the truth of our being. The roots we grow at the crown enable us to sustain the realization of our magnificent potential. It is here at the crown that we embrace the guiding support of divine will to live out our purpose in the world by joyfully creating our life's work as we put to use all of our natural strengths, talents, gifts, and passions.

The *7 Mindsets* cultivates a higher state of awareness that becomes a catalyst for transforming outdated thought and behavioral patterns into new ways of living in this world. Moving up in energetic frequency through the seven main centers of the chakra system allow for the graceful release of aspects of the self that no longer serve an individual's highest good. When we become aware of past ways of being that prevent us from living in our greatest joy, and then intentionally shift to focus on the positive aspects found in those experiences, we literally birth new consciousness unto the planet. The process of awakening to our inner potential wakes us up to the realization that we already have everything we need on the internal realms to deliberately shape a life that is authentic and a true reflection of our heart's deepest longings. By mastering these mindsets, a person becomes a living breathing expression of pure truth.

Activating all of the *7 Mindsets* in this book also assists you in becoming clear as to your purpose in life. As you release past ways of being that do not support who you really are or who you intend to become, you will learn how to shift your awareness to focus on the things that make you feel better about yourself, your life and the current events that you are faced with. Finding new thoughts and feelings that create a more positive, life affirming perspective automatically increase the energetic frequency of the body. As higher vibrational levels are reached, well-being is felt on an emotional, physical, mental and spiritual level. The journey of becoming self-aware not only serves you but the whole of the planet. This is your opportunity to become an active participant in the creation of entirely new levels of awareness that will continue to serve humanity for generations to come. All that is required is for you to start feeling good now!

Where to Begin?

The body is a beautiful sacred chamber for expressing our divine nature. By consciously feeling into the body, we tap into our inner potential and powerful creative abilities using the chakra system as a guide. It is a tool for self-empowerment and manifesting form.

To initiate powerful and sustainable transformation in any area of life is to create a clear channel for spirit to move freely through the energy system of the body so that it may guide and inspire us into action. When moving through the chakra system we begin tapping into the wisdom at the root because this is the center that connects us to the earth and grounds our ability to manifest thought into physical form.

Whenever transformation is intended, it is essential to start at the root so that a strong foundation is set in place from the very beginning.

Identifying Your Starting Point

Knowing exactly where you are starting from sets the cement that holds a strong foundation in place so that you can successfully build from it, sustain positive change, and make quantum leaps toward desired areas of personal growth. When we are not honest or clear about where we are starting from, we initiate transformation from a foundation that is weak and wobbly. Eventually footing is lost on shaky foundations built on false premises. This causes a person to fall back into past patterns that are no longer wanted.

Be honest with yourself about your starting point.

This is where you are currently are at in physical form. Take a look at the situations, the people, and the events that are showing up in your external environment.

- Are certain unwanted experiences continuously appearing in your life?
- Is there something in particular that is missing that you want to create and attract?
- Is there an aspect about yourself that you would like to change and transform?

Becoming clear and honest about your starting point is critical to your success. Identify the area that you intend to transform. Explore the root cause of whatever it is that is drawing your negative attention and draining you of your vital energy. Sometimes it is necessary to go into the pain of your unwanted experiences by feeling into it in order to clearly identify the core issue. For many of us, it is habit to look the other way, make excuses, or mask over situations that are rooted in suffering. The mind does everything in its power to distract us from feeling pain, whether emotional or physical. Since who you really are is beyond the physical limitations of the body and beyond the farthest reaches of the mind, to make powerful evolutionary leaps in your life is to move beyond unwanted experiences and into what is desired. Therefore, it is essential to get clear about what you are facing so that you know exactly where to start from and how to move successfully through it into your desired outcome.

Keep in mind that energy is constantly changing and shifting. Whatever you are up against eventually comes to pass. Know that you have the power and the knowledge to transform any situation into a more positive experience.

Determining the starting point can feel a little overwhelming at times. Too often, we spend a lifetime avoiding the underlying emotional sensations that our unwanted habits and deeply conditioned beliefs create in the body. It does not feel good when a pattern entrenched in lack, survival or fear is triggered. The moment we notice the weight or burden of an undesirable way of being, we immediately go unconscious by shutting down or by finding ways to distract ourselves until the intensity of the pain passes. Resisting or not wanting to face the turbulent emotional storm that is moving through the body causes it to become trapped within one's energy field. The energetic pattern eventually goes dormant as the body continues to hold onto it until it is triggered again at a later time. When old patterns do resurface, and oftentimes with a greater intensity than before, if what is being felt is not acknowledge, honored or seen for what it truly is, the pattern goes dormant again only to arise on another occasion.

If you want to transform the thought and behavioral patterns of old, then it is essential to practice mastering self-awareness and becoming conscious of your unconscious processes. It is said that the subconscious rules ninety percent of a person's day. Since the mind is conditioned at a very young age with the programs and patterns of those we spend the most time with, this means that other people's beliefs are automatically running our life!

It is time to reclaim our true source of power. What we may think or belief about ourselves is most likely based on the programs and patterns that we inherited from other people. To come to know the truth of who you really are is to practice becoming aware of how it feels to reside in your natural state of being. Therefore when we are faced with old beliefs and outdated behaviors, we can tap into the wisdom of the body to gain insight into the true nature of the pattern being presented. With practice, we can determine by feeling into the body whether the experience we are faced with is stemming from the egoic delusions of the mind or if it is rooted in the authenticity of pure truth.

As we become skilled observers of recognizing patterns that are not a true reflection of who we really are, the opportunity arises for one to create new levels of awareness within their consciousness. Shining the light of awareness onto the beliefs and behaviors that limit your capacity to feel good dissolves the power they hold over you. When an individual accepts the presence of their own negatively charged thoughts and emotions for what they are without resistance, they begin to shift.

It is so important to initiate the process of honoring lower frequency sensations as they flow through your energy field. Oftentimes intense emotional experiences reveal vital life lessons that are meant to assist your personal growth and evolution. When we take the time to listen to or sit with whatever it is that wants to be seen on the internal realms, it liberates the stuck energetic pattern. This process is quite similar to listening to a friend in need. Would you deny your friend the support that they are seeking? Most likely, you would honor them by take the time to listen to what they want to express and then you would ask them what they need to feel better. This is the same relationship that our underlying emotional needs request of us. Taking the time to discover what our unseen stuck patterns want to bring to our attention allows it the freedom it needs to release itself from our energy field. A space now opens for something new to be born within us. We become masters of self-awareness when we learn to allow our emotions to move freely through us and acknowledge them for the lessons and blessings they bring that only enhance the journey of our life.

To be honest and upfront with where you are starting from is to allow aspects of the self that have been hiding in the darkness of unconsciousness to move into light. One of the most empowering feelings is to know that you have the potential to create something better in your life, something that serves you and supports your desired direction.

Once the starting point is identified,
the process of transformation and manifestation begins.

Moving Through the Chakras

Now we initiate the journey of moving up to the crown where we reach the apex of thought and enter into the celestial realms of divine wisdom. It is important to move through the individual mindsets as each one acts as a guide for accessing the inherent wisdom of its subsequent chakra. Every mindset builds upon the next and can act as a pedestal for accelerating transformation. Taking the time to explore the principles revealed in each one of the mindsets effortlessly clears out and releases self-limiting ways so that a direct channel to the crown is paved.

When the crown chakra is reached, new insight reveals itself in the form of thoughts, ideas, images, or intuitive knowing. As new thought filters into your consciousness, it makes you aware of opportunities that hold the potential for transforming your ideas, goals and dreams into realized physical experiences. With new found awareness, we begin the return journey back to the root chakra to implement the inspiration received at the crown for manifestation into physical shape and form. This is crucial to our transformation process if we intend to live out and embody the divine insight revealed at the crown.

Moving down through the chakra system and into the root of physical existence, we focus on expanding upon the information discovered at the crown, again, using each one of the mindsets as a guide. By feeling into the essence of the new ideas surrounding your desired way of life, you become a powerful magnetic force for attracting the results that you are aspiring towards. By the time the root is reached, so much time and energy is placed into feeling the energetic frequency of the final outcome that a strong sense of belief and trust in the self's ability to realize the end result is embodied. At this point, you should feel the excitement of anticipation for what is to come. Renewing your commitment to living with awareness of the present moment allows you to stay tuned into moments of inspiration where the inclination to take certain action steps is required to keep the momentum flowing. When we are clear, intentional and purposeful in our actions, our desired outcome begins to take shape and form into our external surroundings with an accelerated speed. The positive emotional states felt on the internal realms are soon to be reflected in the attraction of new experiences and radical changes in your physical environment. At this point, it is beneficial to express gratitude and appreciation for what you do already have, your ability to remain aware of your potential in every moment, and any new changes unfolding in your life.

What to Expect Over Time

Each and every time we travel through the chakra system, we release attachment to our physical body which heals the feeling of being separate from other living things. The mind's incessant chatter lessens as we let go of our investment in the identification with it. Our connection to the inner knowing of our divine source is intensified. This brings the realization that we are not broken or separate and never have been. Indeed, we are already whole, complete, and filled with a constant supply of life force energy that connects us to everything in the universe. Once this knowledge is accessed, we ground the understanding of it into every single one of our experiences. It is through the light of our own awareness that we channel the highest divine inspirations into manifested form. Living with conscious awareness that the essence of who we really are is rooted in the source of divine intelligence, we are able to finally relax into the natural unfolding of our life's journey. This is the mastery that each and every one of us is seeking. Living in the flow of who you really are allows many wonderful and miraculous things to effortlessly exist in your life. Take a journey through the chakra system using the *7 Mindsets* as a guide and transform your way of life. Not only will you experience radical changes in your external environment, you will come to know what it feels like to reside in a peaceful state of total well-being.

The Positive Aspects of Being

Root
Trust
Security
Survival
Safety
Strength
Endurance
Dependability
Power
Identity
Physical Action
Action

Sacral
Creativity
Attraction

Beauty
Worth
Value
Wealth
Pleasure
Relationships
Appetite
Desire
Ambitions
Vitality

Solar Plexus
Joy
Power
Integrity
Self-Definition
Assertiveness
Rejuvenation
Revitalization
Hope
Happiness
Prosperity

Heart
Self-Love
Unconditional Love
Compassion
Purpose
Heartfelt Mission
Passion
Seat of Emotion
Divine Presence
Nourishment
Desire
Acceptance
Forgiveness

Giving
Surrender

Throat
Expression
Communication
Truth
Implementing will
Choice
Freedom

Third Eye
Intuition
Inner Guidance
Seeing
Vision
Awareness
Deserving
Learning
Planning
Dreaming
Goals

Crown
Truth
Inspiration
Wholeness
Completion
Oneness
Universal Consciousness
Self-Realization
Knowing
Wisdom
Appreciation
Divine Presence
BEingness

Root Chakra
- Trust
- Security
- Survival
- Dependability
- Physical Action
- Safety
- Strength
- Endurance
- Power
- Identity

2

"There are two ways to live; one is as though nothing
is a miracle. The other is as if everything is."
– Albert Einstein

❦

The Root Chakra
Location: Base of Tailbone
Color: Red

This chakra connects one physically to the earth by grounding the energy of spirit. It represents ones security, survival, roots, foundations, relationships, stability and structure. A center of physical vitality, the root chakra is a source of power from which one can draw confidence and strength to move through challenging situations. Since this chakra is grounded in the material reality, it is the center of manifestation. When one intends to experience the manifestations of specific outcomes in life, their ability to successfully transform a desired thought form into its physical equivalent is dependent on their ability to channel it through this energy center.

Believe in Yourself!

Many people today are aware of the incredible power of the mind. It is comforting to know that we possess an inherent ability to create whatever we set our mind to. Every one of us has the capacity to tap into this inner resource at will, yet many still do not fully understand how to successfully harness it or where to begin when intending change. The question is how do we effectively co-create with this facet of our consciousness to achieve the results we desire?

The answer lies in the awareness of our thoughts and feelings. Consistently thinking the same thought over and over sends a strong message to the subconscious mind. Repetitious thinking eventually brings one to arrive at the conclusion that they are to receive whatever they have convinced themselves of. When a person comes to accept a series of thoughts as truth, there is also a strong feeling present at the time of the conclusion. The union of thought with feeling creates a deeply seated belief. This is why many people feel so strongly or get so emotionally charged surrounding their beliefs. Once the belief is created, it is handed over to the subconscious mind. Every time a new belief is formed, it becomes the basis from which the subconscious mind executes all future action.

Belief is a powerful state of mind induced through repeated suggestion and subsequent emotions. Our deeply seated beliefs infuse our thoughts with a powerful force of feeling. When a highly charged belief backs one's thoughts, a strong magnetic force is generated from the energy field of the body. The magnetic pull begins to attract more thoughts and feelings that are similar in nature. This begins to expand ones awareness of what is being presented, keeping them focused on the matter at hand. Soon a matching external response eventually appears in the surrounding physical environment actually proving the nature of the thoughts and feelings being projected. It does not matter if what you believe to be truth is actually real or illusionary. If your attention is persistently focused upon a specific outcome, whether positive or negative or whether desired or unwanted, it will ALWAYS show up! This is the overarching natural physical law of the universe, commonly referred to as the Law of Attraction. Once a person is aware of events taking place in their external reality that match whatever it is that they are thinking and feeling on the internal realms, the belief becomes strengthened and the cycle of attraction goes on and on until something different is chosen.

Most of our existing beliefs are formed during early childhood. This means that most of us are not even aware of what our core beliefs are.

Since ninety percent of our day is ruled by the patterns existing in our subconscious, we unconsciously move throughout the day operating from outdated thoughts and behaviors that we have been conditioned with since the time of our birth. These patterns will continue to repeat themselves until we shine the light of our awareness upon them. The moment we stand back and consciously observe our conditioned reactions and responses to certain situations, we create the opportunity for choice. In this moment, we can begin to condition a new response, a new way of perceiving and reacting to the world. The great news is that we can rewrite our beliefs at any given point in time through intention setting, visualization and feeling into the essence of that which is really desired.

Creating new beliefs through repetitious use of affirmative orders can make the natural physical laws of the universe work for anyone. When intending to create change in any area of life, it is important to find the most positive feeling words to describe the desired outcome that you are seeking. Deliberately repeating desired thought patterns and uniting them with supportive emotions as much as possible throughout the course of one's day allows their new way of being to effortlessly dominate the mind. Are you ready for some more good news? As your new thought patterns begin to dominate your mind, they become habit. This means that your desired way of being automatically integrates itself into your waking mentality, making it EASY for you to embody and accelerating your journey to self-awareness!

Implementing new beliefs through repeated suggestion does require a certain degree of disciplined effort, but the reward is well worth it. Not only will you strengthen your ability to hold your focus on the things in life that really matter, you will raise the set points of your body to sustain ever increasing levels of positive energy. Can you imagine living a life filled with a pervasive sense of sheer happiness and well-being? It is so exhilarating and life affirming to feel a constant expansion of joy emanating from within.

Belief is the starting point from which all miracles are created. Without belief, one cannot create or attract the things they desire. Belief must be present when intending to create desired results, for it is the fuel that backs every thought. Since a person creates successful outcomes according to their level of belief, focusing on raising belief in the power of mind will boost one's ability to create and attract desired results with greater accuracy. The following are some effective ways to strengthen belief:

- Deliberately suggest to your subconscious mind your belief in its ability to attract to you the physical equivalent of the directed thought you impress upon it. Make simple clear statements, such as, "I believe in you!" Time must be spent each day directly communicating to your inner mind of your belief in its abilities. Engage the imagination for effective communication of your heartfelt thoughts in the form of words, images and aroused emotion.

- An English Proverb states "the eyes are the window to the soul". Find a mirror, look directly into your eyes and speak out loud to the depths of your soul, where your deep inner wisdom resides. Speak of your admiration, love, respect, and appreciation of its worth. This is a very powerful technique. It will stir great emotion from the depths of your BEING.

- Intentionally arouse positive supporting emotions when stating affirmations. Emotions infuse our thoughts with a vital life force energy. They bring our thoughts to life. Strive to hold positive emotions of well-being as much as possible as you state your affirmations. Feel into them, breathe into them, live as though they are already your reality. Emotions are our sixth sense, our internal navigation system for the course of our life. We sense through emotional well-being how aligned we are to the highest version of our self. When we feel good we are aligned with our true authentic self.

- Focus your intention of strengthening belief in your creative power through art or journaling to anchor your desired thoughts into physical shape and form. Taking the time to focus your intent in this way expresses commitment to your desired goal. This process aligns all four levels of your being

which strongly imprints the subconscious mind and
activates the natural physical laws of the universe.
Your desires will manifest as a result!

Strengthening your belief in the power of you will inspire you to move
forward in your life to deliberately create and attract all the things that you
truly desire with ease and grace. Once a desired goal is fulfilled, you will
find that there are always deeper layers to move through and more desires
wanting to grow, expand and be realized within you. Allow yourself to rise
to new heights. Believe in yourself, the creative potential of your thoughts
and the power of your subconscious mind. Belief is the starting point from
which all miracles happen. Believe in believing.

Affirmations

- I am powerful beyond measure.
- I am the creator of my life experiences.
- I am confident in my ability to create anything I place my powerful focus upon.
- My thoughts and ideas easily transmute into their physical equivalent.
- I strongly believe in the power of my mind.
- I clearly communicate to my subconscious what it is that I desire.
- My subconscious knows everything I need in order to fulfill my direction of thought.
- My subconscious subtly guides me in every moment.
- I have faith in my ability to easily attract desired outcomes in my life.
- I physically act on the inspiration that I receive.
- Every day I take steps that bring me closer to experiencing the realization of my goal.
- I relax in the flow of the universe.
- It is pure joy to allow that which I have set out to create with my deliberate intent to manifest through me.
- Miracles happen when I consciously use the power of my mind.

Ignite Creative Expression with Garnet

Found in mineral deposits scattered across the globe, garnet ranges in color depending on the location in which it is mined. From colorless to rare blue, its most popular shade is a deep maroon. Closely resembling a seed of a pomegranate, garnet is referred to in Latin as "granatus" meaning seed or grain. Dating back to the Bronze Age, 3000 B.C., it is one of the oldest known stones in human history influencing Greek mythology, Egyptian, Biblical and Medieval history.

One of garnets most popular legends dates back to the story of Noah's Ark. It was said that Noah used large pieces of garnet to illuminate the interior and path of the Ark. As a result, garnet has since been a popular stone carried amongst travelers to ensure safety and guidance throughout their journeys.

Garnet has a detailed history in use and lore. One of its most interesting uses was by the tribal Indians in Kashmir. They fashioned it into bullets and fired them at invading British armies. Today garnet is widely used in jewelry for its brilliance. For its durability, it is used as an alternative to sand in the abrasive industry. Its molecular composition and hardness allows it to be efficiently recycled while cutting down on the amount of dust and waste that is produced when smoothing and grinding other material items.

On an energetic level, the glowing luminescence of garnet awakens one to their inherent creative forces. The process of becoming aware of one's creative potential, sparks passion within the self. A symbol of the strengthening effects of light, truth and faith, garnet activates the vitality of life force energy at a root level. As creative expression ignites, the body is energized. This vital flow of energy motivates one to commit to the implementation of inspirational ideas through physical action.

When passion to create is aroused, garnet illumines the path to one's purpose. Its inner glow is symbolic of our desire to create according to our deepest needs. One is drawn to garnet like a glowing warm fire. It nurtures and rejuvenates. Garnet's loving devotion creates a magnetic force that causes a strong attraction to whatever one deliberately focuses their creative energy upon. As a result, instant healing and transformation occur.

A deep gratitude arises for the realization of one's ability to deliberately create according to personal preference. Peace and calm enter the body, as one acquires the necessary patience that allows inspired action to manifest on all levels of being. As self-realization occurs, one grows and expands in their confidence to consciously direct creative expression into any area of their life. Miracles are created.

Wearing and consciously working with garnet activates powerful energies that will have you functioning at peak performance. You can always depend on garnet to light the way. Solutions and multiple pathways will always be revealed. Allow garnet to strengthen your relationship to yourself, your passion and purpose in life. Always look to garnet for comfort and guidance as you create according to your deepest desires.

Questions for Activation

Use the following questions as a guide to further activate this mindset surrounding your intended area for transformation. Be sure to check back in 30 days, 60 days, and at 90 days to reflect on how you much you have progressed and evolved!

Identify the areas in your life where trust is already present.

~

What can you do right now to strengthen belief in yourself?

～

Elizabeth Diamond

What can you do today to celebrate the things in your life that you already trust in and that make you feel safe?

~

If you were to express your heartfelt gratitude and appreciation for all the things in your life that provide a sense of security, what would it feel like?

~

Elizabeth Diamond

What would your life look and feel like if you trusted completely in your inner potential?

∼

Notice if there are any challenges in your life around this mindset. If so, look for the lesson or blessing found at the heart of every challenge. Describe the lesson and how you feel in your body as your awareness shifts to recognize the opportunities being presented for your personal growth.

~

Is there anything else that your inner guidance wants to make you aware of surrounding this mindset?

～

Sacral Chakra
- Creativity
- Attraction
- Beauty
- Worth
- Value
- Wealth
- Relationships
- Pleasure Sensations
- Appetite
- Desire
- Ambitions
- Vitality

3

"Everything has beauty but not everyone sees it." – Confucius

❧

The Sacral Chakra
Location: Navel
Color: Orange

This chakra is the seat of abundant creative energy. It is through this center that one confidently expresses their passions and pleasures in life. The ideas a person has surrounding their self-worth and their ability to creatively express it is channeled through this center. Since the sacral chakra is one of the centers through which emotions are experienced, one can consciously begin to design a life by tuning into what feels best to them. Creating a life that is according to one's deepest desires harnesses the vital energy of this chakra. This center can radiate with a force that is beyond measure. When one learns to channel the force of this center, they will achieve any desired goal that they are seeking.

Abundance Is Everywhere!

Feeling abundant and supported in life is challenging for a lot of people because the mind has a natural tendency to keep a person focused on what is lacking and what is wrong in its attempt to solve the problem. Placing your constant attention on things, situations and events taking place outside of the self can trigger overwhelming feelings of being out of control. It is so important to catch ourselves when we feel this way so that we can find within us the willingness to shift our awareness to focus on the positive aspects present in every situation. When we are able to view our challenges as opportunities, we create the space for new beginnings and pathways to be forged. This is yet another occasion to grow and strengthen our connection to the self.

One unchanging and constant fact is that the only thing a person can control is the way he or she responds and reacts to the life experiences being presented. It is imperative to let go of the need to control anything happening outside of the self as this leads to feelings of despair and helplessness. Instead consciously look for the lesson or blessing in every experience, focus on the positive aspects and remain aware of your personal long-term goals. This will keep you focused on feeling the infinite abundance that is the source of who you really are.

Spend time appreciating the things that you already have and express gratitude for the past experiences that enhanced the overall quality of your life. Waking up to what you do have sends a strong signal to the universe. Any time you want more of something, the most powerful action that you could ever take is to feel a heartfelt appreciation for what is already present in your life. It declares to the universe, "Yes! Yes! This is what I want and I want more of it! This is how I want to feel! This is how I want to live!" It is truly amazing how the simple act of expressing appreciation expands your awareness to see the abundance that is already present in your life. It really is about waking up to what is there and when you do, you will see so many things in your life to be grateful for.

To attract more abundance into our lives, we must first find a way to think and feel more abundantly, to BE abundant right now in this present moment. Be willing to continuously shift your focus to the things already present in your life. Maintaining awareness of this practice will arouse a strong sense of abundance. Seeking the inherent beauty in all things allows one to discover, recognize, and feel appreciation for the abundance of resources currently surrounding you. Sounds easy? It is. The following are a few simple tips to assist in shifting your focus to recognize the boundless abundance that you already possess.

- Reduce the amount of time you expose yourself to the media. Limiting the amount of time you listen to and watch the news will help to keep you focused on what really matters; your positive state of mind and overall feeling of well-being. Although it is important to stay tuned into current events, staying tuned into the programming of the media which is centered on fear and lack, keeps you focused on what is missing and all the things that can go wrong in your life. The news, unless it is a declared positive media network mainly keeps one tuned into and focused on the negative aspects and outcomes of life. Reduce your exposure.

• Clearly state your intentions. Whenever you find yourself focused on what is lacking or missing in your life view it as an opportunity to recreate a feeling of abundance within. Make use of this time to seek out the experiences in your life that positively impact you and make you feel good. Deliberate setting of intentions instantly launches desired thought and feeling in a specific direction, the one that you want! Set intentions to prosper, to thrive, and to discover work that inspires passion. Intention setting empowers a person to feel in control of the way they respond to circumstances and incites productive actions. Declaring positive statements lifts one to the belief that achieving fulfillment of their deepest dreams is achievable. This is the necessary fuel that transforms dreams into a reality. Move forward by setting positive intentions.

• Actively seek out abundance in simple things. Look for and recognize abundance in and around your environment. Abundance is defined as anything in which there is more than enough of. Discovering abundance in the simple things cultivates a master mindset that will ultimately serve to attract more desired experiences of having more than enough. Think abundantly, confirm the abundance already present in your reality, and generate feelings of abundance from within. Remaining disciplined in these actions will allow you to capture the essence of abundance. Experiencing the essence of abundance is the ultimate key to allowing it to flow more freely into your life.

- Be thankful and express your appreciation for all the things and experiences that have already taken place or are already present in your reality. An attitude of gratitude expands your focus to embrace all the positive aspects currently happening in your life.

This planet is filled with an abundant amount of resources. The most abundant resource available to each and every one of us is the creative source of our minds from which all new thought and feeling surface. The birth of new ideas and inspiration create powerful actions that lead to the realization of the abundant experiences that you are looking for. The way in which we think, feel, and choose to perceive the world, can open the door to attracting more abundance into every area of our life. Take the time to feel it NOW! Seek the inherent beauty and positive aspects in every experience. When a person maintains this discipline, abundance is already present!

Affirmations

- I open my eyes to the abundance inherent in all things.
- It is easy for me to see how abundant I truly am.
- I actively seek out abundance in the simple things.
- I am aware of the abundance of resources that the earth has to offer.
- I see the inherent beauty of every moment.
- I am surrounded by an unlimited amount of resources.
- I embrace every experience as an opportunity to expand my potential.
- I choose to focus on the positive aspects in every area of my life.
- I am aware that I must first find a way to feel abundant if physical abundance is to manifest through me.

- ～ Generating thoughts and feelings of abundance allows me to easily attract its physical equivalent into my life.
- ～ I focus on my goals and visions with strength and determination.
- ～ The essence of abundance fills my mind and soul.
- ～ Life is beautiful. I love my life.
- ～ I appreciate and am grateful for all the gifts of the earth.

The Inherent Beauty of Carnelian

Bursting with warm earthly colors, carnelian is a gentle stone that inspires one to identify their unique personal strengths and courage to live life to the fullest. A variant of chalcedony, carnelian is mainly composed of silicon dioxide which is commonly known as quartz. Its color range varies from a pale milky orange to deep rust brown. A reminder of the rising sun, fiery sunsets, autumn leaves and the fertile soil of the earth, carnelian is a symbol of the strength and beauty of our planet.

Carnelian has held a strong presence in the history of the world. It has been found in some of the oldest known jewelry, inlaid into the robes of Pu-Abi, a Sumerian Queen from the third millennium, B.C, among Egyptian tombs, in the breastplate of High Priest Aaron and in many other ancient cultures. One of its most popular uses was by the Romans. They used the stone for cameos, intaglios and as seal rings for imprinting seals with wax on correspondence and documents.

Cool to the touch, carnelian is warming to the soul. Its presence and energetic vibration is calming yet invigorating. Reflective of the stable and nurturing qualities of the earth, carnelian mainly assists one in the birth of new patterns of thought. It strengthens new ideas by holding one's focus upon them so that they can successfully grow and expand into larger concepts. Carnelian helps to keep one grounded in the awareness of their thoughts as it activates a fiery creative energy. The ignition of internal resources creates the inspiration, creativity and courage to discover new ways of viewing life experiences.

Carnelian is a powerful tool to assist one in recognizing resources already present in their life. Shifting awareness to discover abundance that is already a part of one's reality opens the mind to the unlimited possibility of thought. When one fully realizes the transformation that results from refocusing thought, it motivates one to aspire to their highest potential. Viewing life from a new perspective creates the realization that anything is possible. This potentiality inspires the courage and motivation to fully embrace inherent talents that make one unique in this world. Carnelian is effective in assisting one to recognize the inherent beauty of every situation, to view challenges as opportunities and as a catalyst for positive change.

As we learn to deliberately direct focused thought by choosing to see the positive aspects in every experience, we allow feelings of freedom to flow throughout our being. Keeping our awareness on the abundant resources of this planet and our freewill ability to shape our futures through intended thought cultivates feelings of deep love, respect, and appreciation for living. This synergy of thought and emotion are the necessary attractive forces that open the doors to living abundantly.

Carnelian assists us in implementing this message into the totality of our being. Each and every one of us has everything we need in order to survive. All we need to do is just open our eyes, broaden our minds and perspectives to see the inherent beauty in all things. We already possess an abundance of resources. The most abundance source is found within, in the form of thoughts, ideas and inspiration.

The earth is overflowing with resources as well. Look to the earth, it nurtures and takes care of us. Set intentions to stay grounded and remain calm, allow well-being to flow. As carnelian assists us in grounding desired goals into physical manifestation, we can intentionally work with it to create a beautiful life in which we attract life experiences that are according to our deepest passions. From discovering and creating work that you love, to attracting healthy lifestyles and relationships, carnelian brings awareness. Allow it to awaken, nurture, and help you manifest the life you truly desire.

Questions for Activation

Use the following questions as a guide to further activate this mindset surrounding your intended area for transformation. Be sure to check back in 30 days, 60 days, and at 90 days to reflect on how you much you have progressed and evolved!

Identify the areas in your life where abundance is already present.

~

What can you do right now to feel more abundant?

~

What can you do today to celebrate that which you already have?

~

If you were to express your heartfelt gratitude and appreciation for the abundance that you already have, what would it feel like?

∼

What would your life look and feel like if every single one of your needs was fulfilled?

~

Notice if there are any challenges in your life around this mindset. If so, look for the lesson or blessing found at the heart of every challenge. Describe the lesson and how you feel in your body as your awareness shifts to recognize the opportunities being presented for your personal growth.

~

Is there anything else that your inner guidance wants to make you aware of surrounding this mindset?

~

Solar Plexus Chakra

- Power
- Integrity
- Self-Definition
- Assertiveness
- Rejuvenation
- Revitalization
- Happiness
- Prosperity
- Joy
- Hope

4

"Hope is the thing with feathers that perches in the soul, and sings the tunes without the words, and never stops at all." – Emily Dickinson

∽

The Solar Plexus Chakra
Location: Solar Plexus
Color: Yellow

This is the chakra through which one expresses their personal power. With the strength and the ability to radiate like the sun, this center boosts a positive self-image. Pure joy, happiness and a sense of renewal overflow from this chakra. All this encouraging positive energy initiates one to discover the courage to develop personal talents. The inspiration to use one's unique intellect for self-expression in the world places them in alignment with their purpose. It is through this chakra that one comes to deeply accept the self. Self –acceptance allows a deep sense of relaxation to be experienced which is noticeable by the physical act of breathing deeply.

Enjoy Yourself!

Each day, every moment is a new beginning, an opportunity to renew the self. Just as the beginning of a new year or the start of a new season renews a sense of hope, we can view each moment as an opportunity to start fresh, to recommit to the discovery of the empowering sense of being fully aware of the present moment. The pure positive vibration of hope for what is possible in our life is nature's most transforming medicine. Hope energizes the body at a cellular level. Hope invigorates and motivates.

Like an artist sitting before a blank canvas about to create a beautiful masterpiece, we can harness the spark of energy that hope instills to shape a vision for our life by mapping out the days that lay before us. How do you want your life to look and feel like? What beautiful outcomes can you imagine for yourself? Can you make room in your day to immerse yourself more fully into the things that you really enjoy?

Dreaming, pondering and playfully imagining new possibilities allow a person to come to know their true creative ability. The mere act of engaging the imagination to create pictures in the mind unleashes a wellspring of inspiration that motivates one to take action on their heartfelt visions. This is why it feels so good to imagine and to dream about all the things we want in our life. As we create desired scenarios within our mind's eye and feel into the essence of the vision, we align with our pure creative potential. Living out our life goals and dreams as if they are already fulfilled summons a joy that makes one a powerful attractive force for that dream to manifest as a realized experience. Imagination is the vehicle for creating the life we truly want to live. It is the unseen energy that guides the hand to paint a physical reflection of what is being felt and seen on the inner realms to be forever imprinted upon the fabric of the universe. Our imagination creates the story of our life.

As a person spends more time and energy dreaming, imagining and feeling into desired outcomes, the longer they stay connected to unlimited possibility. Anytime one focuses their attention on a desired goal for an extended period of time, the connection grows and expands igniting sparks of inspiration that create a compelling passion for new ideas to be revealed. When creativity flows and a person is in the stream of pure inspiration, motivation is birthed. Taking inspired action from a place of inner alignment ultimately leads to the physical realization of one's heartfelt goals and dreams.

Inspiration is the fire that motivates one to take necessary actions to fulfill their desires. Spending time pondering good feeling scenarios in the imagination initiates inspiration that leads to the creation of new opportunities and adventures. Creating in the imagination is the beginning steps of designing a life filled with all the experiences that one desires.

There is no other time to set your intentions to implement change in your life than the powerful moment of NOW. If our dreams rest in the future, they will always be dreams. Joyfully behaving as if our dreams are already manifested in this moment, right here, right now, creates a strong attractive force. Maintaining a focus on what you really want instead of "what is" attracts desired experiences with an accelerated speed. Yet again, this is a mindset that does require a certain amount of disciplined effort to achieve. The imagination is like a muscle. The more you use it, the more powerful it becomes.

It is encouraging to be reminded that no matter where you may be currently at in your life, right where you are is the perfect place to be. Where you are at, you have never been more experienced, more knowledgeable or wiser than you are in this present moment. There are more than enough resources available to support and uplift you on your journey to self-awareness. From an infinite selection of books, teleseminars, lectures, meet-up groups, podcasts, etc., there are so many sources to choose from to support you as you maintain the necessary awareness that transforms dreams into realities. Make use of these valuable resources. Seek out local groups and people of like mindedness. You will discover that it is easy and effortless to fully realize the experiences that you are imagining for yourself.

Here are a few other suggestions to keep you feeling a sense of empowerment:

- Each morning upon waking, set your intentions for the day. Renew personal affirmations and visualize yourself living out what you are affirming as though it has already happened. Talk yourself up by using the most positive and uplifting words you can find. Tell yourself how powerful you are and that you can create anything you set your mind to. This self-affirming talk instills a joyful hope of all good things to come throughout the day. It puts you in a positive mindset that attracts more experiences that are like in nature.

- At some point throughout the day, write down three inspired actions that you are willing to commit to in order to bring you closer to achieving a desired goal. The goals that you choose should feel easy and fun. We are not looking for quantity here, only quality. Remember, it is all about feeling the joy of creating out of passion and inspiration. Only create goals and steps that feel good and bring joy to your day.

- Anchor your dreams and visions by giving them physical shape and form through a visual platform such as vision boarding, creating a mind movie, or intentional scrapbooking. The Intentional Scrapbooking Method™ is a meditative process that contains all the creative elements that strongly imprint the subconscious of desired direction. Scrapbooking with focused intent allows all four levels of being to move into alignment. This sends a crystal clear message to the universe of the desired outcome you intend to achieve.

- Upon falling asleep at night, ponder your accomplishments of the day. Taking the time to recognize your achievements places you in that enjoyable spot of where you want to be which creates a powerful attractive force. Allow yourself to spend time living out your desired dreams as you drift off to sleep.

When we learn to embrace each moment as a new beginning and bring a rich powerful presence to it, we persistently renew and strengthen our commitment to the self. We become an active participant in the story that is our life. Embrace the statement, "The present moment is the only time there is!" Each moment of every day is a fresh, new beginning to be celebrated with a vital sense of aliveness and an intensity of hope for all the beautiful things unfolding in your life. What wonderful things are you imagining for yourself?

Affirmations

- Every moment is a new beginning, a fresh start.
- I joyfully choose to focus upon thoughts that make me feel good.
- It is easy to focus on the things that I desire.
- I am confident in my ability to create and attract anything I place my focus upon.
- I enjoy creating on purpose.
- Happiness is a decision, I choose happiness NOW.
- Happiness radiates into all my actions.
- Hope energizes my entire being.
- I have never been more wise, more knowledgeable, and more experienced than I am in this moment.
- Living is a delightful experience.
- I enjoy life.

The Renewing Effects of Peridot

Formed in the depths of volcanic activity, peridot is one of the few gemstones that occur in a single color: green. A species of Olivine, its color range ultimately depends on how much iron is contained within the crystal structure. More abundantly found in a translucent yellow-green color, peridot is more rarely found in its gem quality color of olive green. It is mined in many locations across the globe, although the highest quality specimens come from Myanmar, Pakistani and Egypt. Peridot has extraterrestrial origins as well. It is the only stone found in meteorites. The Hawaiians refer to it as "Pele's Tears". Pieces of peridot are frequently found scattered among the black sands and lava rocks on Hawaiian beaches.

Peridot's radiant color has caught the fancy of humans for many years. It is estimated that this gemstone has been mined for over four thousand years. Frequently found in Egyptian jewelry and amulets, historical legend states that peridot was the favorite stone of Cleopatra and that some of her so-called Emeralds were in fact peridots. The ancient Romans nicknamed the stone "Emerald of the Evening" for its ability to maintain its brilliance in any kind of light. Found in medieval churches and referenced in the Bible to be one of the stones lain within the breast plate of the High Priest, peridot periodically enjoys being at the height of the fashion industry whenever green is declared to be the color of the times.

The brilliant light of peridot aids healing and well being at the mental, emotional and physical level. It is extremely effective at subduing matters of the heart. Peridot's soothing energy allows one to accept "what is" with a calming forgiveness. One can use or wear peridot to relieve mental anguish, depression and anger and to revive happiness, inspiration and hope.

The yellow hue that expresses itself through peridot rejuvenates and warms the soul. Like the sun shining through a window on a beautiful day, peridot motivates one to wake up to their inner hopes and dreams. It stirs a positive expectation for all good things to come. The hope that peridot awakens, energizes the entire being at a cellular level. As the inherent yellow hue within peridot directs its energies into the solar plexus, it aids one to implement inspired hope into physical action.

Peridot's renewing energy brings clarity to one's goals. It joyfully encourages one to act on their heartfelt goals by unleashing the inspiration that offers solutions to one's search. As one begins to align with their true purpose, a joy for living is regained.

Allow peridot's warm and friendly nature to renew your joy for living. Open to the stimulating energy of hope that will strengthen and rejuvenate your entire being. Peridot provides the energy boost that effortlessly lifts you into action. Now, you can begin to really enjoy the process of living according to the divine plan. Infuse an abundant amount of radiant energy into your life and daily activities by including peridot in your life.

Questions for Activation

Use the following questions as a guide to further activate this mindset surrounding your intended area for transformation. Be sure to check back in 30 days, 60 days, and at 90 days to reflect on how you much you have progressed and evolved!

Identify all the things and activities that you enjoy the most.

~

Elizabeth Diamond

What can you do right now to create more room and space in your day to engage in the activities that you enjoy the most?

∼

What can you do today to celebrate the things that fill you with joy and well-being?

~

Elizabeth Diamond

If you were to express your heartfelt gratitude and appreciation for the things that bring you the most joy and well-being, what would it feel like?

∼

What would your life look and feel like if you completely immersed yourself in activities that you truly enjoy every day?

~

Notice if there are any challenges in your life around this mindset. If so, look for the lesson or blessing found at the heart of every challenge. Describe the lesson and how you feel in your body as your awareness shifts to recognize the opportunities being presented for your personal growth.

~

Is there anything else that your inner guidance wants to make you aware of surrounding this mindset?

Heart Chakra
- Self-love
- Unconditional Love
- Compassion
- Divine Presence
- Nourishment
- Acceptance
- Forgiveness
- Surrender
- Giving
- Desire

5

"You yourself, as much as anybody in the entire universe, deserve your love and affection." – Buddha

✍

The Heart Chakra
Location: Center of Chest
Color: Green or Pink

This is the chakra of unconditional love and compassion. It is through this center that one experiences the sensation of their heartfelt feelings. The heart chakra is the center that connects one to identify with other people, animals, plants, and forms of life. This is the most sensitive and vulnerable of chakras. Because it is the center of the entire chakra system, when balanced and open, energy is able to effortlessly flow back and forth to the other chakras which allows the whole being to be filled with its loving energy. When one is filled with the loving energy of the heart chakra, its healing energy radiates outward into ones environment.

Love Yourself First!

Expressing and receiving love is one of life's greatest delights. Allowing the frequency of love to fill every fiber of your being literally makes the physical heart cavity feel full and complete. Love is a powerful emotion that instantly heals on an emotional, mental, physical, and spiritual level. Its resonance uplifts and transforms one to a higher energetic vibration. Every human inherently possesses a strong desire to feel loved and accepted. It is essential that one comes to the understanding in their life journey that the only real basis for obtaining a true sense of security in the world is to consciously become aware of the love that flows from the divine source present within. Once realized, a person can tap into its vast reservoir to fill every atom of their being with its infinite supply. Achieving a deep sense of personal fulfillment is possible when one practices loving and nurturing the self first.

It is natural to crave the peace and contentment that love offers. The enduring inner craving is the gentle calling of our higher self to connect with the divine loving source from which our being was created, to remember who we really are. The ability to go deep inside of ourselves, align with source energy and consciously tap its eternal well-spring of love is a freewill decision. Voluntarily choosing to replenish ourselves with the love that flows from within creates a strong foundation for inner peace and self fulfillment to blossom. As one starts to implement self-love into their daily practice, a deep sense of calm begins to overflow into the words and actions of one's personal reality.

Learning to nourish and take care of the self in the moment as needs surface, one develops knowledgeable skills that allow them to more effectively help other people. Once a person understands how to create emotional stability through self-love are they able to give love to others freely and unconditionally. There is no other person that you can look to for a continuous supply of love and support than yourself. You will always be there for you! You know exactly what is needed in every moment to bring emotional well-being and stability into your life.

Capturing and embodying the true meaning of love enables your very presence to be healing for others to be around. Filling the self with love on a daily basis creates a channel for love to flow into every action. A person is extremely magnetic when their being radiates this high vibration. Others are naturally attracted to those who express self-fulfillment, because they understand how to effectively communicate from the heart. Speaking and acting straight from the depths of the heart allows its pure intention to be felt. The joy of being able to freely share information and to give to others unconditionally is the purest expression of love.

Oftentimes, many of us seek external sources of love to fill the empty void felt within the heart center. We seek attachment to people and things outside the self in order to provide a sense of security. As things and people consistently change with time, we discover that we cannot control anything that happens outside of the self. Expectations we place on others to fill the void within most often leads to disappointment. It is only the self united with the eternal flow of love from the unlimited source within that a solid foundation is built for one to effectively accept and adjust to all of life's consistent changes.

There are many ways to begin initiating the process of filling the self with love. It is a life long journey of self-discovery, to love where you are at and to love where you are going in every moment. The following are a few suggestions to help get you started:

- Set the intention every day to allow the loving energy of source from which you came to fill your heart and every fiber of your being. Seek out a quiet space and breathe deeply. As you breathe in, visualize loving energy in the form of light enter through the top of your head. As your breath fills your diaphragm, bring the loving energy into your heart center. Keep doing this until your heart feels full and complete. Let your imagination be your guide!

- Reaffirm your self-worth on a daily basis. Know that you deserve the best in every situation. If something does not feel right or good to you, take the time to sit quietly with the experience and listen to the wisdom that wants to emerge. All inner guidance that surfaces from the divine source within you is always positive in nature. Do not accept anything less. You deserve the best. You are worthy of feeling good in every moment and in all situations.

- Look into a mirror and express your heart-felt love for yourself. Tell yourself of your beauty and your worth. Speak of your appreciation for all the experiences you have had on your life's journey. Know that you would not be who you are in this very moment without them. Listen intently as you allow every cell of your body to soak up the feel good statements of love being uttered from your lips.

- Trust yourself! You are your own best guide! You know exactly what you need in every moment to create peace and well-being. Take care of your needs first before attending to others. When you feel nourished, then you are ready to give freely and unconditionally to others.

- In times of intense challenge, allow your feelings to flow through you. If you feel like crying, please do! Crying helps to release emotional trauma. Let the tears flow and be gentle with yourself.

- Be forgiving of yourself. Forgiveness heals when you allow yourself to BE no matter what you are feeling in the moment. Forgiveness is pure acceptance which releases any resistance to the present moment. Forgiveness also releases the accumulation of suppressed internal wounds of the heart. Nourish and comfort yourself by expressing your forgiveness of past memories and feelings. Let them go and move forward. Let love fill its place.

Loving the self before all things is a rewarding process in the journey of personal awareness. Take the time to go within and create a lasting relationship with the well-spring of source energy from which all love flows. The love that stems from the self is unlimited and expansive. You will be forever replenished with an unending supply of love as you consciously tap into its current. Allow the true meaning of love to fill you and then freely express it. Love's overflowing presence within you will uplift the world. You will LOVE yourself for it.

Affirmations

- I am aware of the loving presence of source energy that is present within me.
- I intentionally choose to fill my heart with love.
- I breathe deeply as I visualize love penetrating the chambers of my heart.
- I am devoted to nurturing myself.
- I know that when I take care of myself first, I can more effectively help others.
- I always remember to love myself.
- I listen to my heart and follow its voice.
- I cherish the presence of love in my life.
- I allow love to overflow into all my words and actions.
- I radiate pure divine love.
- I delight in the sensation of love.
- I am in love with love.
- I love the journey and the experience of living my life.

The Divine Loving Essence of Rose Quartz

A long standing symbol of love and beauty, rose quartz is the most desirable variety of quartz crystal. A gemstone used over the ages mainly for ornamental purposes, its color has remained somewhat of a mystery to scientists even to this day. Rose quartz's color is completely unique. Unlike any other pink mineral specimen, it's color ranges from light pink to a deep rose red and has recently appeared on the earth sporting a slight lavender hue. Mostly opaque in form, rose quartz can also manifest itself as transparent. The transparent gemstones are frequently fashioned into jewelry.

Scientists believe that the color of rose quartz is a result of a combination of iron, titanium, manganese and even colloidal gold impurities. Recent studies performed under micro analytical methods have discovered the color to be a reflection of unknown microscopic mineral fibers. These tests suggest the possibility of a totally new and yet unknown fibrous mineral. The color of rose quartz is photosensitive and can fade if placed in direct sunlight.

Found mainly in the cores of large pegmatites as solid masses of rose colored quartz, its individual crystals have poorly formed boundaries. This adds to the mystery of rose quartz as quartz crystallizes into well-formed crystals in all its other macroscopic varieties. Because rose quartz was once believed to be only massive, when discovered in a crystal structure, the first ones were dismissed as fake by mineralogists from around the world. Currently, Brazil is the only true source of rose quartz found in well formed crystals. The beauty and the rarity of rose quartz specimens found in crystallized form are extremely valuable. Rose quartz in its massive form is mined mainly in Madagascar, India, Germany and the United States.

There is little known historically about the uses of rose quartz. Pieces of the gemstone have been discovered in jewelry of the Mesopotamian, Assyrian and Roman cultures that date as far back as 2000BC.

Although rose quartz has been valued over the years for its ornamental beauty, it has a deeper meaning and purpose for manifesting itself on our planet. At first one is attracted to the beauty of its sweet pink ray. As one moves into direct contact with its energetic field, its calming vibration and intent is immediately felt. Whether or not one is aware of its powerful healing abilities, rose quartz immediately begins to emit its gentle loving ray into the chambers of one's heart.

Its penetrating energy begins to circulate within the heart center, releasing suppressed feelings and emotional traumas while reinstating the gentle loving forces of self love. As it begins to release unbalanced energy, negative emotions are replaced with the soothing essence of divine love. One will experience the sensation of relief as rose quartz allows the flow of love to comfort and soothe past experiences that were previously filled with sorrow, fear and resentment.

The intense vibration of rose quartz teaches the true meaning of love by guiding one inward to connect with the eternal divine source from which all love flows. As one begins to learn that true love comes from within, rose quartz assists in reprogramming one to nurture the self through forgiveness and self-love. It is from this inner source that all emotional traumas no matter how deep or painful are healed.

Rose quartz is an intense healer for those who feel they have never had love given to them. People who feel unloved and have never encountered experiences of receiving unconditional love most often lack a joy for living.

Not feeling worthy, feeling lonely and holding a negative self-image will continue to attract equivalent experiences into one's life. Rose quartz heals past conditions and programs that have been accumulated from birth as it reprograms the heart to love itself.

Here are some suggestions for working with Rose Quartz:

- When feeling emotionally unbalanced or moving through a challenging experience, get a piece of Rose Quartz and wear it on your body. Be sure to run it under water to cleanse it after each use.

- To allow its healing energy to effortlessly reprogram your heart with its inherent divine message, place a piece of rose quartz under your pillow at night while you sleep.

- The hand that you write with is your dominate, giving side. The other is the receiving side. On days that you would like a boost in the expression of giving love, wear a piece of jewelry that contains rose quartz or slip a piece into your pocket of the dominant side of your body. On days that you would like to experience the influx of receiving more love, wear a piece of rose quartz jewelry or place a specimen in your pocket on the non-dominate side of the body.

Rose quartz manifests the vibration of infinite self-love like no other crystal on this earth. At last with rose quartz one can begin to experience a true sense of inner peace and self- fulfillment. As the heart is nourished and healed from within, a deep comfort flows throughout one's being carrying the message that all is well. Rose quartz in all its mystery is a channel for divine love to flow. It is up to you to allow its presence to remind you of who you really are.

Questions for Activation

Use the following questions as a guide to further activate this mindset surrounding your intended area for transformation. Be sure to check back in 30 days, 60 days, and at 90 days to reflect on how you much you have progressed and evolved!

Identify all the ways that you nurture and replenish yourself.

~

What can you do right now to fill yourself with more self -love?

What can you do today to celebrate the love that you already have?

~

If you were to express your heartfelt gratitude and appreciation for who you truly are, what would it feel like?

~

Elizabeth Diamond

What would your life look and feel like if you nurtured your needs first before attending to others?

～

Notice if there are any challenges in your life around this mindset. If so, look for the lesson or blessing found at the heart of every challenge. Describe the lesson and how you feel in your body as your awareness shifts to recognize the opportunities being presented for your personal growth.

Is there anything else that your inner guidance wants to make you aware
of surrounding this mindset?

~

Throat Chakra
- Expression
- Communication
- Truth
- Implementing Will
- Choice
- Freedom

6

"A good laugh is sunshine in a house." – William Makepeace Thackeray

∽

The Throat Chakra
Location: Base of Throat
Color: Blue

The center of communication, the throat chakra enables one to calmly, clearly and freely express their ideas and feelings. When this chakra is balanced and opened, one possesses the desire to speak of the realization of their inner truth and connection to spirit.

Laugh Often!

Let's face it, everyone benefits from a daily dose of laughter. It is no joke that laughter is good for a person's overall health and well-being. Laughter is a physiological reaction to an inward state of joy. The emotional release that it provides signals acceptance and connects people to one another. Laughter is a social activity that is instantly contagious. It only takes one person to initiate a wave of laughter that lightens the overall mood of a group. So what is it that makes laughter a natural pathway to enhance physical vitality and happiness?

Laughter is instant transformation. Negative thoughts and emotions cease to exist when laughter is present. In fact the brain stops thinking entirely! During times of challenge, studies have proven that if a person finds it within them to laugh at the matter at hand, it dramatically shifts their perspective from negative to positive. Not taking life too seriously allows you to be more at ease with your present environment. Approaching challenging situations in a playful manner is more conducive to creative problem solving. Not only is laughing productive in helping a person to shift their focus, it gives the diaphragm and the upper body a great work out. Exercising in this manner relaxes the muscles, increases endorphin levels, and boosts the immune system.

Studies also show that people who laugh often are able to sustain lasting states of happiness. In turn, they are rewarded with longer life spans, better health and subsequently attract larger amounts of money than those who move through life unhappy. Feeling happy is a direct reflection of our divine essence and laughter is the key that opens the gates for joy to flood into our life experiences. Laughing truly allows a person to feel the inherent joy and freedom that is their divine birthright. This is naturally expressed in babies who learn to laugh before they speak. Children that are born deaf and blind possess the same natural ability to laugh. In truth, everyone is capable of laughter and we all laugh in the same way. We are all connected by our ability to laugh. Laughing is the sunshine of the soul and when expressed, it creates an increase of joy being felt on the planet that everyone can benefit from.

Obtaining an increased level of happiness is achievable right NOW. Laughter is one of nature's best medicines and it is free! You can achieve a greater amount of happiness and laughter in your life with these following suggestions:

- Set the intention in the beginning of the day to actively seek out reasons to laugh. Starting the day in this manner suggests the anticipation of good things to come. The expectation of a positive mental state activates immediate physiological and emotional responses. This leads to the release of endorphins that flood the emotions with joy and well-being. When you fill your mind with happy thoughts and feelings at the start of the day, you will be sure to attract many experiences that that are equivalent to the nature of your dominant intent. This is deliberately putting the natural laws of the universe to positive use.

- Make a point to get together with a group of friends on a daily basis. Instead of focusing on problems, make it a point to act silly and giggle. Play games, dance or share funny stories. We have a natural tendency to enjoy sustained periods of laughter when we are in comfortable environments amongst friends. Studies show that we laugh harder and longer when we interact in groups than if we were to watch something funny in a movie or on TV.
- There are institutions and instructors that specifically focus on teaching the art of laughing. Laugh clubs and laugh yoga groups are becoming more and more popular. Seek them out and find out what they have to offer.
- Spend time with children. They overflow with laughter. It is said that children laugh up to 400 times a day. Children are a natural testament to the truth of source. They intuitively know that play and laughter are vital to feeling good. Since it is our birthright to freely experience the joy of being, children are the purest expression. Have you ever noticed that witnessing a child belly laugh brings a smile an instant smile to your face? Join the fun by playing with kids and be sure to participate in a game of chase so you can laugh too.
- Remember a time that you could not stop laughing. Focus on it until you get the giggles. Notice how easy it is to arouse joy by remembering a hilarious moment in your life.

Allowing more laughter into your life is a decision and like optimism it can be learned. When a person chooses to experience more laughter and actively seeks it out, they begin to appreciate the profound positive effect that it has on the emotions and physical body. Aligning with the joy and freedom that is ones natural birthright through laughing uplifts others in the process. It is amazing how the joy of laughter provides more meaning and purpose in one's life on many different levels. Open the door to the abundance of life by laughing often. Laughter is a short cut to easily achieve all your desired dreams. Imagine what you can create by choosing more joy and laughter to flow into your life experience in this very moment. Laughter opens the heart and sets the spirit free. Now is the time to live life laughing.

Affirmations

- Laughing opens my heart and sets my spirit free.
- Laughing and feeling happy is my true state of Being.
- I utilize my natural freedom by choosing to laugh.
- Every day I set the intention to actively seek reasons to laugh.
- I experience laughter in abundance.
- A good belly laugh fills my soul with sunshine.
- Laughter allows the sunshine of my soul to brighten all existence.
- Laughing renews strength and balance in my self- expression.
- Laughter enhances my physical vitality.
- Laughter makes my heart shine brightly.
- The sweet sound of laughter attracts joy and abundance to me.
- Laughter attunes me to the divine perfection of the universe.
- Laughter is an uplifting vibration that increases the amount of joy on this earth.
- Laughter makes life a pleasant journey with a happy ending.
- Laughter is the sunny side of existence.
- May my soul eternally erupt with laughter.

Expressing Truth with Chrysocolla

A gemstone that instantly reminds you of beautiful mother earth, chrysocolla is the ultimate symbol of balance and well-being. It looks like the earth as viewed from space with its sky blues and greenish blue to green colors. Often confused with popular Turquoise, chrysocolla is a mineral of secondary origin, a by-product of copper ore. Mainly located in arid climates such as Armenia, Macedonia, Spain, Arizona, New Mexico and Mexico, it occurs in the oxidized zones of copper mines. Chrysocolla manifests itself in solid veins, rounded masses, or globular, bubbly crusts that can range from dull to waxy or glassy to opal-like in appearance.

True chrysocolla is extremely soft and fragile and cannot be used in jewelry. However, when it agatizes with quartz to form a chalcedony, chrysocolla increases in hardness to match the durability of pure quartz. Often times as it merges with quartz, its chalcedony version takes on a beautiful and unique translucent gem quality which is commonly referred to as Gem Silica. Chrysocolla can also be found covered with a crust of miniature sparkling quartz crystals that is referred to as druzy that is beyond exquisite.

Chrysocolla has an interesting history of use. It was discovered that chrysocolla could be formed artificially by steeping ore during winter and then evaporating the liquid with the heat of summer. Countries such as Spain would use the material formed from these batches to create the most vivid colored paints for artists. It was also entered into an index of recommended medicines to be used as caustic applications for sores, wounds, ulcers, and even as an emetic.

The principle use of chrysocolla and the origin of its name were discovered by Theophrastus in 315 B.C. It was given the name from the Greek words *chrysos,* meaning "gold" and *kola,* meaning "glue", because its first use was to solder gold. Chrysocolla was the most popular material to use in the soldering of gold because it produced the brightest and highest quality alloy.

Aside from its stunning physical characteristics, chrysocolla has a direct energetic effect on the heart and throat centers. As soon as one comes into contact with this beautiful stone, a sense of peace and calm penetrate the body to the depths of the soul. It is as if the endless possibilities of the sky combine with the strength of the earth and the depths of the oceans to harness the unlimited potential of this stone. Because this crystal represents a harmonic balance of earthly and etheric energies merging as one, a message that "all is well" is implemented on a subtle level. The soothing energies of chrysocolla enable one to clearly recognize their alignment to the overflowing well-being of source energy.

Attuning to the divine harmonic frequencies of the universe allows ones inner truth to surface so that they are better able to clearly recognize the perfect words to express it. This alignment dissolves lower frequencies and negative vibrations. As anger, sadness, grief, resentment and other negative thoughts are released from the physical body, relief is evident. After the heaviness is lifted one is able to relish in their new found lightness. The glorious sensation of feeling fluid, free and uplifted activates an inner resolve to speak from a place of empowerment clearly communicating positive truths. And finally, one is able to allow the truth of their being to shine through in the expression of joy and laughter.

With chrysocolla at your side, you sit in awareness of the divine expression present in all things. This stone opens the heart and calls forth the truth of your character. Let it clear the blocks that prevent you from freely expressing yourself in this world. Feel the freedom to claim joy and happiness in every moment and live accordingly. Chrysocolla harmonizes your energy field with its balanced energetic frequencies gently caressing you into the gliding current of the universe. Allow it to inspire you into powerful self-expression so that you may actively participate in uplifting our planet.

Questions for Activation

Use the following questions as a guide to further activate this mindset surrounding your intended area for transformation. Be sure to check back in 30 days, 60 days, and at 90 days to reflect on how you much you have progressed and evolved!

Identify the areas in your life where laughter is already present.

~

What can you do right now to fill yourself with more laughter?

~

What can you do today to celebrate the things that make you laugh and feel the freedom that is your natural state of being?

~

If you were to express your heartfelt gratitude and appreciation for the sense of freedom experienced when communicating your deepest truth, what would it feel like?

~

What would your life look and feel like if your day was filled with ubiquitous amounts of laughter?

~

Notice if there are any challenges in your life around this mindset. If so, look for the lesson or blessing found at the heart of every challenge. Describe the lesson and how you feel in your body as your awareness shifts to recognize the opportunities being presented for your personal growth.

～

Is there anything else that your inner guidance wants to make you aware of surrounding this mindset?

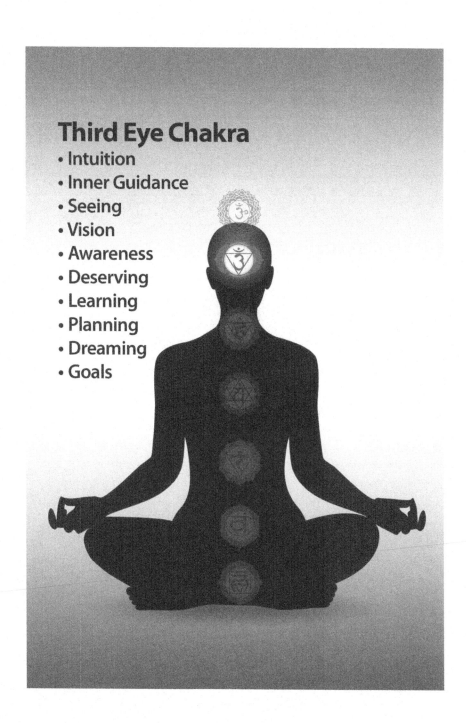

Third Eye Chakra
- Intuition
- Inner Guidance
- Seeing
- Vision
- Awareness
- Deserving
- Learning
- Planning
- Dreaming
- Goals

7

"Imagination is more important than knowledge. Knowledge is limited. Imagination encircles the world." – Albert Einstein

∽

The Third Eye Chakra
Location: Between the Eyebrows
Color: Indigo

The center for higher guidance and intuition to develop, this is the chakra of personal awareness. As one becomes more aware of the true nature of the self, courageously embraces it and then powerfully lives it, they align with their highest potential. It is through this chakra that one has the ability to transform self-limiting thoughts of ego into positive statements of truth. When one fully realizes their deepest truths, they effortlessly merge with the infinite source of creative energy to fulfill desired dreams. It is through this chakra that a person becomes conscious of the power of maintaining a present awareness.

Seek Clarity!

Never is a person more clear about what they really want in life than when they go through an undesirable experience. Yet it is the natural tendency of the mind to keep you focus on what is not wanted in its attempt to figure it out! Unwelcomed experiences often trigger a surge of negatively charged emotion which releases a powerful magnetic force that continues to attract more of the same types of occurrences. As the universe always responds to match the energetic tone being offered, a person can get stuck on a continuous cycle of attracting one unwanted experience after the next. The next time you find yourself stuck repeating an unfavorable chain of events it is time to get clear as to what you do want.

Clarity is the cornerstone of every desire. We all want solutions to our challenges in life. In the process of looking for answers, whether it is in regards to relationships, work, money, health or business, we are inclined to search outside of the self. We call on our friends, families or experts. We look to books, search engines, classes, or seminars for guidance. Sometimes we find what we are looking for and sometimes we do not. And more often, we encounter solutions that provide only temporary relief. It is not long before we find ourselves back where we started. Again, we begin searching outside of the self for another quick fix or magic pill that offers a short lived respite from the on-going cycle of adversity.

The point is that we are conditioned to seek external means to solve our internal conflicts. The next time you are in need of answers to your life's challenges, resist the urge to exhaust your vital resources by searching the periphery, instead, dive deeply into the root of your existence. If you are ready to sustain powerful positive change in your life, then it is time to turn within and tune into your personal source of inner guidance. The divine source available within you is eternally present and infinitely greater than our limited individual self and when asked always reveals the correct wisdom, insights, and answers every single time.

To summon the guidance of divine wisdom, all one has to do is ask and the answers appear. A person can use a process called creative visioning to open the communication channel and at the same time stimulate the flow of clear insight from the most profound source of their consciousness. Valuable information is always communicated back and forth through the imagination. It is through this vehicle that we successfully communicate to the source of our inner guidance and it communicates back to us. Once we clearly understand the communication channel between our imagination and our divine source, we can effectively harness this connection to transcend any challenge.

Creative vision is the act of using the imagination to image a scenario of a specific desired outcome. It is like creating a movie in your mind, where you live out the role of the hero celebrating the successful outcome of the desired end result that you intend to manifest in your life. The more time spent engaging the imagination by feeling into the essence of the outcome, the clearer the direction is given as to what you want the end result to be. The process of creative visioning stimulates the release of guiding insight from the wise and all-knowing source present within you which ultimately leads to the physical fruition of your desired outcome.

The question is how does one recognize authentic guidance when it surfaces? Answers reveal themselves in a variety of ways and appear in their own unique time. From an entirely new idea, to an inner hunch, or a flashing inspirational thought that guides you to take a specific form of action, the imagination is an indispensible tool that must be trusted in order for its communicative ability to become stronger and clearer. The more we trust the information that surfaces and consequently, take the necessary steps to place it into action, our ideas begin to have an accumulative effect as they build upon one another. Before long a series of connections are made that highlight the relationship between the two elements, where you currently are and the solutions that lead to where you want to be.

The more time spent focusing on a desired outcome enables it to grow clearer and clearer. It is when we become crystal clear as to what we really want that our inner guidance increases in intensity by making us more aware of the opportunities that lead to the end result that we are looking for. Oftentimes, the solutions are already in front of us, yet we were not made aware of them until we asked for guidance. Creative visioning is like creating a map, where a direct course or even a series of routes are made known leading to a desired outcome. There may be multiple courses of action that you can take that will lead to the result that you are seeking. It is all about choosing the one that feels the best to you.

Whenever new insights surface, it is important to pay attention to the thoughts that surround it. Frequently, ego based thoughts simultaneously arise from the mind to analyze, criticize, doubt and even dismiss the information surfacing from our inner guidance. It is common at first to blow off the guidance being received. We are conditioned at an early age to not trust the imagination, to view it as child's play. Before you dismiss any new thoughts or ideas as a mere figment of your imagination, there is a more subtle way to tune into the authenticity of the guidance being received.

With each new impression surfacing into your awareness, there is always a corresponding feeling that accompanies it. As you become more present with and in tune with your body, your thoughts and your feelings, you will begin to notice how you feel in your body in response to different types of thoughts. There is a notable difference in the quality of feeling triggered in the body as a result of wisdom surfacing from your authentic source of inner guidance than thoughts stemming from the ego based mind. Tuning into how you feel in response to what is surfacing allows you to confirm the authenticity of the guidance being received. The quality of feeling that arises when guidance is streaming from your true authentic source is like an electric jolt of energy. It holds a raw vitality, a sensation of excitement and aliveness that charges you up and is intended to inspire you into action. Often times right after we experience this initial response, the egoic mind kicks in to tell you all the reasons why you should not listen to this guidance as it plays it off as ridiculous and insane. These thoughts suppress the initial supercharged feeling of being vitally alive causing you to come to a standstill. Words rising out of the egoic mind are heavy literally making the body feel weighted down and burdened.

The best way to disarm the over reactive mind when searching for solutions from your inner guidance is to practice being an observer. Standing back and not attaching meaning to the guidance surfacing, you can objectively observe how your body feels in response to the new ideas you are witnessing. As you come to know the difference between the true authentic guidance from the divine source within and the false information stemming from the critical ego based mind, you will become clear as to which direction to take. Noticing an electrifying sensation united with a brand new thought or idea is the authentic inner guidance that you are looking for. Any thought that is fear based, negative or critical in nature and tends to weigh you down surfaces from the egoic mind.

When a person practices tuning into the feeling response of the body, they awaken to an awareness of an inner navigational system. It is just like having a GPS system in a car. In order to move from A to B, one must give clear direction as to where they intend to go if they want to receive clear direction as to how to arrive at the desired location. Developing the ability to receive clear guidance from the divine intelligence that flows through all living things requires a willingness to nurture that connection. A stable channel must be created in order to allow the communication to flow clearly and with ease. Recognizing this amazing aspect of your being can deeply enhance your journey to self awareness.

The following are a few suggestions to strengthen your connection to the source of your inner guidance so that you can more clearly communicate:

- The next time you need solutions to your life's challenges, try tuning into your inner guidance first before looking for external means. Getting into the habit of doing this strengthens the connection. You will be amazed at how quickly answers appear to your questions once when you make it your practice to look to yourself first.

- When asking for guidance, clarity is key! If we cannot see, sense or feel the details of the end result, we are not clear as to what we really want therefore the guidance will not be clear either. When you are clear as to what you want, be willing to ask your inner guidance for solutions in such a way that exclaims, "Yes! This is what I want in my life! Show me the way!"

- Entertain the fulfilled outcome! Sometimes our imaginative abilities have become weak due to lack of use, yet this powerful ability can be brought back to life through stimulation and exercise. Deliberately holding the focus on a desired scenario works out the muscle of your imagination. As you bring your imagination back to working order, this fertile platform will help you grow and expand all your dreams.

- There is something to be said about the process of journaling and letting ideas flow. If you find that you are challenged surrounding the details of your desired outcome, try journaling. Not only does writing down your vision crystallize the clarity, it begins the process of anchoring your ideas into physical shape and form. It gets the ball rolling so to speak and often times with an accelerated speed. The great thing about journaling is that you can look back at what you wrote and almost every time, what was written has already become a realized fact in your life.

- Surrender to the timing of the guidance that you are looking for. There is a natural timing for things to unfold, guidance cannot be forced. Sometimes we are not quite ready for the answers to reveal themselves, yet they will show up when we are truly ready to receive them. You have awakened something deep within you, it will surface. Answers always appear in some form.

- It is all about deeply listening to whatever it is that wants to emerge. Breathe, be still and hold the space for guidance to gently surface. Resist the temptation to grab onto what is emerging or the urge to attach meaning to it. Be willing to take action on whatever enters into your awareness to keep you moving forward in the direction of your desired outcome. Keep in mind that every insight has an accumulative effect. So no matter how small the direction, always be sure to follow it to express your commitment.

As we strive to align with our highest potential, we can summon the profound wisdom of our inner guidance to light our way. The more we become clear as to where we intend to go, the more we become aware of the opportunities that will guide us there. New ideas and inspiration are infinite in scope as they flow directly from the creative source that permeates everything in this universe. The imagination is the channel through which all new ideas are handed over to man. It is up to us to nurture this connection, to ask, to listen, and to take positive action on whatever wants to emerge in our life. Small steps of inspired action are the necessary fuel to transform any desired dream into a reality.

Affirmations

- The creative potential of my thoughts is unlimited.
- I nurture my dreams by envisioning them.
- I powerfully create with each thought.
- I focus upon my visions with mental and emotional clarity.
- Creative insight speaks to me in the form of my imagination.
- I clearly communicate what I intend to create.
- Enduring powerful mental focus is easy, fun and effortless.
- As creative insight surfaces, it inspires me to ascend.
- I am conscious of my thoughts.
- I clearly see my purpose in life.
- My conscious awareness is the sacred key that unlocks hidden wisdom from the depths of my soul.
- I align with my greater purpose with grace and effortlessness.
- I recognize and allow the subtle impulses of my inner guidance to inspire me into action.
- I claim my destiny in every moment.

Into the Depths with Lapis Lazuli

A stone so ancient, it is said to have existed before time itself, lapis lazuli is a powerful stone for awakening awareness within the self. Abundantly found throughout the ruins of many ancient civilizations, it was highly prized by the Egyptians and Mesopotamians. Used as a tool for raising consciousness, lapis was highly revered for its ability to bring wisdom, truth and light to the user.

The oldest known sources that produce this semi-precious material are the mines of Badakshan province in Afghanistan. Relics and talismans found among ancient civilizations are traced back to this known source for the past 6,500 years. Although it can be found in other locations across the world, these mines produce the highest quality specimens.

Lapis lazuli is comprised of a deep cobalt blue with scattered flecks of highly reflective golden pyrite. Its intense color is such a contrast to the dry and arid land of the desert in which it is mined that one can understand its prized popularity since the dawn of time. A known spiritual tool, lapis had many other purposes. Due to its saturated color it was frequently pulverized into powders to be used as paint, dyes, healing poultices, and eye shadow, as worn by the infamous Cleopatra.

Lapis Lazuli is one of two crystals in the mineral kingdom known to penetrate and surface rather than heal. It is most effective when placed on the middle of the forehead just between the eyebrows. This location is frequently referred to as the third eye. When placed here, it subtly assists the user in the release of limiting beliefs and false illusions of the self by shinning the light of awareness upon them. The deep blue color resembles the dark vastness of the ocean while the golden specks of pyrite are like piercing beams of light illuminating its depths. With lapis lazuli, we immediately enter the cosmic current of the universe and experience the flow of who we really are not through the thoughts of the mind but in the presence of BEingness. The piercing golden rays of light stir the awareness. Subtly, energy begins to move as outdated ways of being are released so that a space opens for a crystal clear pathway to the divine to be forged. Once the communication channels are open, the inner wisdom of the soul is revealed through vivid images, deep insights and resounding sensations via the gateway of the imagination. The true nature of our inherent inner wisdom that was once lost and forgotten over time is now again realizing itself. Lapis quickly draws a person into the depths of the infinite intelligence of their divine source.

Working together, lapis lazuli connects one to their personal source of inner guidance to powerfully and forcefully focus on desired visions with precise clarity. As dreams grow and expand in the eye of the beholder, divine insight reveals the necessary steps that fulfill a desired goal.

Lapis not only aids in surfacing clear insight, it shows a person certain actions that they may need to perform in order to ascend to higher levels of being. This means that it reveals any information about what is blocking, preventing or standing in the way of achieving a desired goal. Lapis brings to light any and all thought patterns and emotional wounds that need to be released and healed. In other words, when someone is finished working with lapis, they will have a clear understanding as to what they really need to accomplish in order to turn their dreams into a reality.

Allow the deep blue ray of lapis to carry you to the depths of your inner guidance where you can access the brightly shining truth and wisdom of your being. Lapis is a vehicle through which we can truly experience the light of the higher celestial realms and implement the wisdom received by expressing it into physical action.

Questions for Activation

Use the following questions as a guide to further activate this mindset surrounding your intended area for transformation. Be sure to check back in 30 days, 60 days, and at 90 days to reflect on how you much you have progressed and evolved!

Identify the areas in your life where clarity is already present.

~

What can you do right now to become more aware of your connection to your source of inner guidance?

~

What can you do today to celebrate the times that you tuned into and listened to your inner voice which ultimately led to successful outcomes in your life?

∼

If you were to express your heartfelt gratitude and appreciation for your personal source of inner guidance that reveals profound wisdom every single time when asked, what would it feel like?

What would your life look and feel like to know exactly what is needed in every moment to maintain a state of optimal well-being?

∽

Notice if there are any challenges in your life around this mindset. If so, look for the lesson or blessing found at the heart of every challenge. Describe the lesson and how you feel in your body as your awareness shifts to recognize the opportunities being presented for your personal growth.

~

Is there anything else that your inner guidance wants to make you aware of surrounding this mindset?

~

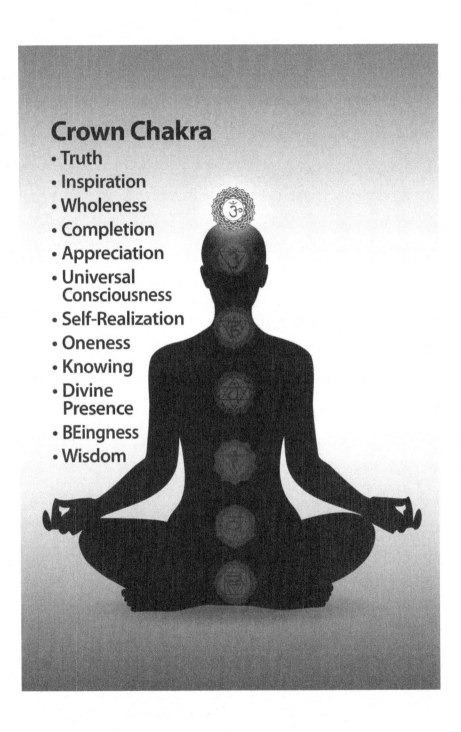

Crown Chakra
- Truth
- Inspiration
- Wholeness
- Completion
- Appreciation
- Universal Consciousness
- Self-Realization
- Oneness
- Knowing
- Divine Presence
- BEingness
- Wisdom

8

"When you become conscious of Being, what is really happening is that Being becomes conscious of itself." – Eckhart Tolle

❧

The Crown Chakra
Location: Top of the Head
Color: Violet

This is the center of higher consciousness where there is no separation between self and spirit. It is in this chakra where one fully realizes the illusion of physical reality and embraces the realization of the omnipresent and ever expansive nature of divine presence within.

Be Present, BE Yourself!

It is extremely common in our culture for people to lead very fast paced lifestyles. Always on the go, moving from one thing to the next, we keep ourselves busy searching for the next best thing. We have become experts at multi-tasking ceaselessly looking for a means to the end. It is so easy to pursue things that instantly gratify and entertain us rather than make an effort to explore new avenues that could ultimately instill a lasting sense of fulfillment and purpose that is long term. As a society we have become impatient. Entitlement has become a dominate thought pattern among many individuals, who think that just because they are alive, things should be handed to them. When a person's needs are not instantly met, they become frustrated and sometimes angry. Our time and energy is tied up in the pursuit of material things and pleasurable physical experiences. As a result, there is a pervading sense of never being fully at ease, rested, or relaxed. The peace that is eternally present at the core of our being is hidden because we have become consumed by things occurring outside of the self.

It is normal to identify with the mind because that is where we literally experience the physical sensation of our consciousness. The mind is invested in associating with things going on in our external surroundings to ensure our security and survival in the world. It is consumed by fear, lack and loss and is always striving to define itself in the world. Perceiving reality through identification with thoughts and words arising from the mind is to invest in a false sense of self. Because we perceive the physical world through the five senses, it is easy to convince ourselves that what we are interpreting and thinking about is fact. In reality, the truth about who we really are is so much more than what we think about ourselves or how we identify with our physical form. We are eternal consciousness that can only be completely grasped and fully understood by feeling the natural state of our being. BEingness in no way can be encapsulated or totally described by words. To attach thought and meaning to it is to limit its infinite and expansive existence. Comprehending the wholeness of your true divine essence is to practice sitting with yourself in present awareness. Allow yourself to dwell in the stillness of pure BEing and you will become aware of your divine nature, your oneness, your connection to the whole of all things living.

To acquire this knowledge, it is essential to tune into the deep peace present at the core of your existence. This is easily achievable when a person takes the time to deeply relax the body and the mind simultaneously. Once a person is capable of stilling the mind and quieting the body are they able to activate an awareness that reveals the existence of an inner presence that is greater than the self. Taking the time to experience deep relaxation, one begins to heal the feeling of being separate which is the root cause of all pain and suffering. Tapping into the infinite wholeness of the divine presence that flows through you and all living things puts the building blocks in place to realizing who you really are. When you entertain the quiet stillness and listen to what is already present within you, a space opens for grace to enter.

BE willing to see beyond the self-limiting thoughts of the mind by releasing the heavy burden of its words. The profound presence of peace is discovered in the spaces between the words and thoughts of the mind. When you spend time getting to know what it feels like to dwell there, to exist there and allow yourself to be present in the knowing of it, the sensation expands. Developing this practice creates a solid foundation for peace to emerge into every aspect of your life.

- You can do this right NOW! Stop thinking about the past and stop anticipating the future. Having your thoughts scattered in these places prevents you from experiencing the rich splendor of living in the present moment which is the most powerful place that one could ever reside in. Collect all of your awareness right here in this very moment by calling back all parts of you. Stay present and grounded in a strong sense of self as often as possible. Everything becomes possible when you live and create in the present moment.

- Take a few moments a couple of times every day to breathe as deeply as you can. Become aware as to how your body feels in response to your breathing. When we focus on our breath, we immediately tune into a state of present awareness. It instantly resets the body and slows down the thought processes so that we can enter into a state of clarity. Breathing deeply allows new life force energy to fill our entire being.

- Meditate! This is the key to relaxing deeply. Let go of any expectation, clear the mind and enter into a space of peace and quiet, a place of not knowing and deeply listen to whatever it is that wants to unfold in your life. Meditation is the most important daily discipline or habit that you could ever develop. It is the only practice that enables you to experience the silence that ultimately establishes a connection to the divine presence within you.

- Honor your emotions by letting them flow through you. Try not to resist them. When we resist how we are feeling, our emotions become stuck within the energy field of our body. We will continue to experience them over and over again until we learn how to allow them to just BE. Everything that happens in our life must be honored for what it is. Practice observing your emotions as if they have space around them. Emotions are a movement of energy. All things eventually come to pass, try your best not to seek yourself in what you are feeling by attaching meaning to your emotions. Let them be, let them flow.

- Try not to cling, attach, or grab onto specific outcomes or goals. Remember it is all about relaxing into the flow of your life and allowing a natural organic unfolding of events to take place. Set your intentions clearly surrounding the things you feel the most passion for and then enjoy the journey of arriving at the desired outcome however it wants to unfold. This is much easier and way more enjoyable than trying to force outcomes to happen! Keep in mind that everything takes place according to its own divine timing.

- Right NOW is the only time to BE yourself. Make a commitment to spend time in the presence of you. Get to know the true authentic you! You are magnificent!

Let go of the need to fight, to struggle, to be consumed by the accumulation of things and just BE! Surrender to the presence in you that is still and at peace so that all of a sudden you discover a space in which there is room to breathe. Tapping into the presence of something larger than you that is divine in nature allows you to experience the lightness of BEing. Feel it, know it, and sense its truth within your heart. You may not be able to physically see it or touch it but you can always feel its truth resonating throughout every fiber of your body. When we begin to awaken to just how full and complete we already are, we accelerate our awareness of the self. Seeking serenity in the spaces inbetween our thoughts enables you to sit in the presence of the highest version of you. Listening to this quiet still place stirs the soul for new ways of being to emerge in your life.

The mind will always be there to return to. Get to know your divine authentic self, sense it, be aware of its peaceful presence and then intentionally call forth its light to infuse every waking action. External things always come and go, but a true sense of self is always present. Nurture this connection so that you can fully embrace its expression. When you arrive at a place where you realize that you do not need anything else that is outside of the self, that is when you will finally be able to enjoy the journey of becoming more than you ever knew was possible. Your life will unfold in profound and meaningful ways.

Affirmations

- ~ I AM.
- ~ I am whole and complete.
- ~ I am aware of the divine presence within.
- ~ I stand in the light of my awareness.
- ~ I allow the light of the divine presence within to infuse every action I choose to take.
- ~ I know the truth of my being.
- ~ I am in the flow of my life.
- ~ I honor what is.
- ~ I allow emotions to flow through me with ease and grace.
- ~ It is easy for me to enter the silent space that exists in-between my thoughts.
- ~ I deeply listen in silence.
- ~ I know the possibilities of my soul.
- ~ Who I really am emerges from the stillness present at the depths of my being.
- ~ I enjoy the journey that is my life as it unfolds naturally and organically.

~ I exist in the present moment.

~ I am at peace everywhere I go and in all situations.

~ Everything is possible when I shine the light of my awareness upon it.

Open the Gate to Higher States of Awareness with Amethyst

A stone traditionally associated with royalty and spiritual leaders of antiquity, amethyst continues to be a popular stone among spiritual seekers. A purple variety of quartz, its regal color makes it a stone of high demand. Worn as a mark of rank for hundreds of years, it is an abundant mineral found in many locations across the globe. Amethyst manifests itself in a variety of unique structures that are particular to certain regions or mines. Available in a wide range of shades, the rule of thumb is that the deeper the purple color, the higher the grade, the more valuable the stone. The most notable quality of amethyst is found in the mines of Brazil, Uruguay, Russia, Africa, and Ontario.

Its name comes from the Greek word *"amethystos"* which literally means not drunk. Amethyst's name originated from the lore of Greek Mythology. There are different variations of the tale from which it deemed its name although the basic premise consists of a story between the god, Dionysus, and a beautiful woman, Amethytos, who was trying to escape him. In an attempt to save her, the goddess, Artemis, turned her into a white stone. In Dionysus's remorse, he poured wine over the top of the stone staining the crystals purple. Since then, the Greeks believed amethyst to be an antidote for intoxication. In order to prevent it, they would drink wine from challises carved out of the stone.

Besides roots in Greek lore, amethyst has been a favorite stone among rulers over the centuries. Found scattered among the many tombs of Egyptian royalty and the Anglo-Saxon graves of England, amethyst was believed to contain mystical and superstitious powers. It was largely employed in antiquity for use as intaglios and worn as amulets. The Russian Empress, Catherine the Great, loved amethyst so much that she sent thousands of miners into the Urals to bring back as much as they could carry. Leonardo da Vinci once wrote that the gem dissipates evil thoughts and quickens the intelligence, an insight that must have surfaced from working directly with the stone.

On an energetic level, amethyst is a stone that assists one to successfully experience states of inner awareness. It gently instills a profound tranquility to the mind that quiets everyday habitual thought processes. For people who desire to achieve a state of serenity through meditation, yet find it challenging to enter the stillness, can easily transform from one reality to another with the aid of amethyst.

Attuning to amethyst is like being handed a golden key that opens a gate to higher consciousness. Its peaceful vibration has such an immediate calming effect on the emotions and physical body, that one is able to effortlessly experience a deep state of physical relaxation. Achieving peace of this magnitude, a person is able to easily let go of past thoughts, beliefs, and self-centered notions. In the letting go of illusions of what one believes to be real, transformation occurs. Amethyst opens the mind to usher in a wisdom that flows directly from the infinite divine source. As it floods into ones consciousness, a deeper understanding of one's purpose for living brings clarity to the divine universal forces at work. As the mind begins to grasp the existing presence of an intelligence that is greater than itself, it is able to embrace the concept of a higher self. This awareness activates one's ability to trust in the guidance that arises from within. Knowing that one is equipped with an inner navigational system, they are able to intuitively grasp the essence of true peace and well-being, a harmonic state that was present at the time of and before birth.

Receiving wisdom of this nature profoundly inspires one to redefine their belief in what is possible. Once a person aligns with the truth of their being, they discover a renewed zest to transform areas of their life that are not in alignment with the new knowledge that they have acquired. As new ideas surface as to how one can begin shaping a life that is according to what they really desire, amethyst assists in the process of transforming self-limiting or self-defeating thoughts to more productive ways of thinking. Amethyst then carries the direction of the newly formed thoughts and ideas created during the imaginative process of dreaming to the depths of the soul where it is implemented.

With amethyst, the opportunity to shift into expanded states of awareness is within your reach. Allow the calming effects of the purple ray to calm your mind and bestow peace upon your soul. You will achieve an awareness of self that you never knew was possible. Let the universe fill you with its wisdom and guide your course. Reside in the flow of eternal freedom.

Questions for Activation

Use the following questions as a guide to further activate this mindset surrounding your intended area for transformation. Be sure to check back in 30 days, 60 days, and at 90 days to reflect on how you much you have progressed and evolved!

Identify the areas in your life where peace and well-being are already present.

~

What do you need to do to on a daily basis to begin saying "yes" to whatever life throws your way, to surrender to it and fully embrace it?

~

What can you do today to celebrate the divine expression that you are?

~

If you were to express your heartfelt gratitude and appreciation for the divine intelligence that resides within you, what would it feel like?

~

What would your life look and feel like if you lived in complete awareness of the present moment?

~

Notice if there are any challenges in your life around this mindset. If so, look for the lesson or blessing found at the heart of every challenge. Describe the lesson and how you feel in your body as your awareness shifts to recognize the opportunities being presented for your personal growth.

~

Is there anything else that your inner guidance wants to make you aware of surrounding this mindset?

∼

9

"Wonder is the beginning of wisdom." – Greek Proverb

∾

Wake Up! Face Your Consciousness with Eyes Wide Open!

Images of skulls are everywhere we look these days. Printed on sneakers, clothes, stationary, all types of art, and many other popular products, skulls are everywhere. Even the latest *Indiana Jones* movie is based on a legend regarding the abilities of ancient crystal skulls. What is the current fascination with the image of a skull?

While popular culture associates skulls with Halloween and death, to the ancient civilizations of old, the image of a skull symbolized a desire to move into a higher state of awareness. To them, it was a figure that literally represented the shape of the human head, the physical part of the body that holds the brain. Through this organ, one physically experiences the awareness of their mind and all of its activity. Many ancient civilizations utilized and honored the image of a skull as a sacred symbol for knowledge and wisdom. Not to be mistaken for literary or academic knowledge, but to be understood as a great inner knowing that resonates as truth deep within ones being.

There is a reason for the surfacing of the skull symbol as a modern day fashion trend. It is a sign that our civilization as a whole is moving toward the achievement of higher states of personal awareness. The spiritual wave sweeping across the planet has caused many people to question the purpose of life and their meaning in it. Little by little, more and more people are awakening to the awareness of what it means to live consciously.

The collective desire of our modern day civilization to acquire a deeper knowledge, to awaken to consciousness, shows up as an attraction to images of skulls. The ancient meaning of the skull symbol has been encoded into the cellular memory of our DNA since the beginning of our evolution. From generation to generation, its meaning has been passed unrecognized in the collective unconscious of humans. A strong collective desire to uncover the truth of one's existence and purpose in life is currently revealing itself through a resurgence of skull images.

For those who are aware of the deeper meaning behind a skull's symbol, they can intentionally use its image to accelerate the awakening process.

- One way to consciously work with the image of skull as a tool for personal transformation is to bring a representation of it into your physical presence. Since skull images are the latest fashion trend, it is extremely easy to find many beautifully designed images marked on material goods. Find an image that attracts you and meditate upon its deeper meaning. Imagine the types of thoughts the ancients experienced when working with the symbol. Allow your imagination to carry you back to a time when this image was highly revered and considered sacred. Engaging the mind in this manner will allow inner wisdom to surface from the collective unconscious through the vehicle of your imagination. Performing this exercise will enable you to acquire a deeper understanding of the benefits gained when moving through life with conscious awareness.
- Conscious awareness has been represented since ancient times in the form of crystal skulls. Currently, there are a handful of known crystal skulls that were once used and revered in ancient civilizations. Discovered through archeological digs, the

most well known crystal skull that was properly referenced in the recent *Indiana Jones* movie is the Mitchell Hedges skull. There are an abundance of contemporary skulls carved from many varieties of crystal available today. Purchase one and carry it in your pocket, meditate with it or even place it under your pillow at night. You will be amazed at the depth of insight that it can call forth within you.

Our society overflows with an abundance of skull images. Explore the profound meaning behind the resurgence of this once sacred image. Learn how to use this symbol to summon your inner wisdom so that you may better understand the purpose of life. Take a journey with the image of skull. It will open your eyes to the awareness of your consciousness.

Crystal Skulls as a Tool for Awakening to Consciousness

Crystal skulls have been used since the dawn of time as a tool for awakening and expanding consciousness. Used by civilizations of old, crystals in the shape of a skull are a powerful tool for awakening self-awareness today. Energy studies have discovered that crystals shaped into a skull image take on a different more complex set of characteristics than if left in natural form. Crystals that are carved into skulls dramatically increase in vibrational frequency. As soon as a crystal begins to take on a rudimentary form of a human skull, the energetic field of the crystal rises to encapsulate a synergistic compilation of information. This means that as a crystal is being carved into a skull shape, it begins to combine the collective consciousness fields of the human kingdom, the crystal kingdom, and that of the crystal skull. What results is a combined energetic field of three different consciousnesses. When intentionally brought into ones personal energy field, it activates the collective consciousness of crystal, man and the crystal skull simultaneously.

Crystal skulls are storehouses of information. Their energy field contains the knowledge of all human experience collected since the beginning of time. This information which is already present within each and every one of us is stored in the unconscious sphere of our consciousness, oftentimes referred to as the Akashic Records. Although a person may be unaware that they possess this type of information, crystal skulls assist in the surfacing and remembrance of it. Since crystal skulls contain the collective consciousness of three separate energetic fields, they instantly link one to consciously access the wisdom of the ages.

Crystal skulls gently and subtly draw us into the depths of our consciousness where we attune to and align with our natural state of being. They assist us in waking up from the dream of our attachment to and identification with the false limited sense of self. As we begin to awaken to our true reality and spend time sitting in the presence of who we really are, the illusion of our physical cloak begins to dissolve. All of a sudden we realize that our strong identification to the mind and our physical form is the root cause of all our pain and suffering. At last we become conscious that we are eternal consciousness that is as deep as the oceans and as infinite as the sky. Once we recognize that we are pure consciousness itself, our ability to sense, to feel, to know the eternalness of our being is strengthened. This is when we begin to withdraw from the illusion of being separate and merge into wholeness of who we really are. Consciousness realizing itself is experienced when we enter into a space that is so vast and expansive that its pure feeling fills us to the core of our being with a sense of profound peace, fulfillment and completion. When we sit in the presence of the infinite I AM, it magnifies our awareness of it. We become so deeply rooted in the understanding of it that every action becomes infused with its knowing. This is the truth of our Being. This is freedom.

As you increase in the awareness of your consciousness, you will realize the unlimited potential you inherently posses as a human being. A desire to acquire more knowledge is ignited and that thirst is the necessary fuel that moves one to ascend into higher states of awareness. When you live in alignment with a knowing of your greater purpose, deeper insight into the meaning and purpose behind creation is continuously revealed.

A crystal in the shape of a skull is a metaphor for awakening to consciousness with eyes wide open. Crystals are already highly reflective in their natural structure, but when they assume a skull form, they actively mirror the recent state or existing level of one's own consciousness. Being able to "see" where you are presently at in your current level of consciousness allows you to "see" yourself for who you truly are. It is crucial to have a true sense of where you are starting from, so that you can be clear as to where you intend to go. A crystal skull can guide you to face aspects of yourself that require transformation so that you can harmoniously and more fully embrace your true divine state of being.

Crystals naturally record and store information, yet a crystal shaped into the image of a skull records and stores information with a stronger sense of magnification and acceleration. Reflective of mankind's unique consciousness, a crystal skull is filled with the potential of unlimited possibility. To intentionally combine your consciousness with a crystal skull is to take your personal potential to greater heights. With both consciousnesses activated, you can achieve higher levels of wisdom and understanding contributing to the evolution of our race.

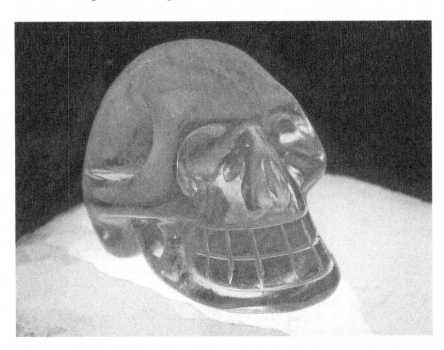

Successfully Activate
and Program Your Crystals

10

"Everything that exists has Being, has God-essence, has some degree of consciousness. Even a stone has rudimentary consciousness; otherwise, it would not be, and its atoms and molecules would disperse. Everything is alive." – Eckhart Tolle

༄

Successfully Activate and Program Your Crystals

Crystals used since ancient times as a tool for raising consciousness are also responsible for our modern day technologies. Crystals not only lend their earthly beauty as ornamental pieces and jewelry, they possess extremely high rates of vibrational frequencies enabling them to broadcast energetic information.

Birthed into existence within the depths of the earth, the intense light that a crystal naturally displays is not realized until it moves out of the darkness and into the light. This process gives us insight into their purpose on the planet. Their radiant light and balanced frequencies can be a catalyst for bringing our unconscious processes into the light. They release the weight, the burden of unconsciousness with ease and grace. Behind every adversity of dis-ease, disorder, loss, or struggle, there is a lesson to be recognized and integrated into our way of life. Crystals help us to see the blessing in every experience. Self-healing begins when a person is willing and ready to transform. A person can facilitate and accelerate the process through the use of crystals.

Crystals also act as catalysts for lifting us to reconnect with our whole complete self, the divine presence within so that we regain full remembrance and awareness of it. Because of their intense ability to express light, when we clear our mind and open our hearts to attune to their message, they speak directly to our inner knowing through subtle impressions. They show us how to stand strong in our own inner light, how to radiantly let it shine forth into our actions, and how to better express it in unique and creative ways. Awakening to higher states of consciousness, we align with the truth of our being. Crystals amplify the realization of our deepest truths. They lovely reflect back a conscious knowing of the infinite potential of our creative abilities.

We can also use crystals as a tool for manifesting our highest purpose in this world. As a person intentionally merges their awareness with that of a crystal, the two consciousnesses become one. The crystal will amplify the intention and project the information in the form of thoughts, feelings and images into the farthest reaches of the universe like a radio tower. The intensity in which the information is projected is greater than the self or the crystal alone could emit. This act of co-creation helps to fulfill the purpose of both the individual and the crystal simultaneously. In this way we support each other's intent while serving the highest good of the planet by creating a more loving, peaceful and harmonious world.

How do crystals assist in transformation?

Each crystal encompasses different functions and characteristics that are uniquely expressed in varying ratios throughout the wide range of specimens displayed in the mineral kingdom. This is due to the crystal's unique molecular structure, clarity and color that it manifests. The major functions of crystals include; their ability to record, store, reflect, amplify, and transmute information in the form of sounds, images, thoughts, emotions and even scents. Crystals actively work to bring harmony and balance to every environment. This means that they naturally absorb unbalanced energies of lower vibrations, such as negativity, transmute them into higher frequencies, and then project the synchronized energy back into the surrounding environment. Crystals are so committed to this purpose that they willingly trade their life force in order to bring harmony to any environment.

Any information that a person intentionally initiates and builds upon through focused thought and feeling is capable of being released into a crystal. As the crystal itself is activated, it absorbs any energetic information that it comes into contact with. The crystal naturally increases the quality of the information it accumulates through a natural amplification process. It then begins to broadcast the stored program into the environment in waves of high vibrational frequencies.

What is so unique about co-creating with crystals in this way is that they intensely project the energetic essence of our desired outcome into the surrounding environment on a continuous basis, all day long. This ultimately gives us the freedom to focus on other things. In fact, it is impossible for a person to hold a steady stream of focus on a specific outcome for an extended period of time, yet a programmed crystal can. We can utilize the powerful abilities inherent in crystals to help us create the life of our dreams. Let them assist you as you focus on your desired goals and visions. Can you feel the love, the joy, the freedom that they offer? Appreciate their inner light and physical beauty so that they can lovingly reflect back to you the splendor that already surrounds you from the inside out.

Imagine the Possibilities

As human beings, it is in our nature to want to shape a life that reflects what we truly desire and feel the most passion for. Crystals are the blossoms of the mineral kingdom helping us to awaken to our full creative potential. They express themselves unto this earth and into our lives so that we can more fully realize our true purpose.

Begin to think about what you want to create and attract in your life. Use your imagination and begin to daydream about an ideal outcome. Pretend that you are truly living it out in this moment as if it is happening right now. How does it feel? What does it look like? What are people saying? Is there a smell? Use your imagination to engage all your senses. Mentally and emotionally unite with your desired experience and live it out!

In the realm of imagination anything is possible. Right now as you sit in the essence of what you intend to create in your life, the experience of it is already a reality on a mental and emotional level. Let's focus your intention further by anchoring it into a crystal. Let the crystal absorb your intention, thoughts, emotions, and images of your fulfilled end result to assist you in the attraction of what you truly want!

Programming Your Crystal in Five Steps

1. Choose your Crystal

The crystal you choose to create with is always the right one for you. The source of your inner wisdom is always guiding you on a subtle level. It knows everything you need to bring your entire being into a state of wholeness and well-being. You will be guided to the crystal that perfectly aligns to your current level of awareness. Most often you will experience a resonance of knowing deep within as you connect with the crystal that is meant for you. With your inner guidance leading the way, you can be sure that you will always choose the right one.

2. Cleanse Your Crystal

To make sure your crystal functions at its peak level, it is essential to cleanse the crystal of any lower energetic frequencies it may have absorbed during its journey into your life. It is important to cleanse each and every crystal before co-creating with it.

There are many ways to cleanse a crystal. Some highly recommended and preferred methods are to place a crystal in sunlight, moonlight, saltwater, and even bury them in the ground. These are all very effective ways and all contain one key ingredient: INTENTION! With that said, to cleanse a crystal is to use intention. Close your eyes and as you declare the following statement aloud or in your mind, "I am now cleansing this crystal of any negativity", imagine a radiant ray of light shining forth from the core of the crystal dissolving any and all lower vibrations. Crystals also benefit from contact with water. I like to hold my crystals under a source of running water, such as the kitchen sink, while stating my intention and visualizing the light. Bringing a crystal into contact with the element of water instantly allows it to realign at an atomic level. Negative and lower energies are immediately released.

Make it a point to cleanse your crystals whenever you think about it. They speak to you through the imagination! Every now and then, I place my larger, heavier crystals in the shower and let them bathe for a few minutes. They love it! Once you cleanse a crystal using intention and water, you will sense a shift in their vibration. They literally look brighter to the eye and feel more alive in your hand!

3. Activate Your Crystal

To awaken the inherent energy of attraction within a crystal, hold it firmly in your hand. Crystals are always cool to the touch when first picked up. Take the crystal in your hand and allow your awareness to touch the crystal. To do so is to begin by appreciating its beauty. Then open your heart to it by recognizing the expression of the divine presence within it, the same one that is also present and simultaneously flowing through you. Deliberately intend to co-create with it. Together you can manifest your desires with ease and effortlessness.

Now it is time to begin stimulating and activating the pyroelectric and piezoelectric energies of your crystal by firmly pressing down on its physical structure in a rubbing motion. The applied pressure excites the electromagnetic field which heats the crystal. As the crystal warms up, the physical structure expands and the electromagnetic energy attracts the surrounding information present in the environment into itself. It will begin to store and record energetic information in the form of thoughts, images, sounds, and emotions. The activated crystal has been known to attract even small pieces of physical matter such as dust or sand into itself. To test the temperature of the crystal, touch it to your cheek. If it is warm to the touch, it is properly activated.

4. Project Your Intention into Your Crystal

With focused awareness, declare your intention as you continue to apply firm pressure to the crystal. Once the intention is stated, it is time to begin the process of relaying information into it. Feel into the essence of your desired outcome as if it is already fulfilled and you are currently living out the experience of it. For this step, I have found that it is extremely relaxing and effective to lie down placing your crystal either over the third eye or heart chakras.

When programming the desired outcome into the crystal, be sure to give it all you've got! There is no limit to your imagination. Place the overall feeling, using every emotion, sound, word, predicted taste or smell, into the experience of what it feels like to live out the end result of your desired outcome.

Hold the focus on feeling into the desired experience for as long as you can. If you find that your thoughts are beginning to wander, it means that your focus has reached its peak. As your mental images and aroused emotional state begin to fade, know that you are complete in programming your crystal. The crystal has recorded and stored the essence of the desired experience and will continue to amplify and project the energetic frequency of that which you intend to manifest and realize on a consistent and steady basis.

5. Remain in a State of Positive Expectation

Now that you have successfully programmed your crystal, it is time to relax into a state of positive expectation. Release attachment to the outcome, resist the urge to control it, just know that it will unfold in its own natural time. It is kind of like ordering a pizza. You place the call and then know that it is on its way. There is no need to control how it is made or how it will arrive, but when it does you thoroughly enjoy the outcome. So relax into a knowing that positive results are going to manifest at the perfect moment. When you recognize signs, no matter how big or small, that the universe is shifting to fulfill your request, express your joy and appreciation. Maintaining a state of positive expectation supports the energy that you generated through your intention. Whenever you find yourself thinking about the end result of your desired outcome, allow positive thoughts and eager anticipation to fill your entire being. By doing so, you can be sure that you are consciously choosing to sustain the energy that you placed forth in the highest manner.

Now comes the fun part! It is time to take your crystal and place it where you can view it frequently. Each time you view the programmed crystal it acts as an anchor to reaffirm and reinforce the feeling of your desired outcome. Remember to relax into the knowing that fulfillment of your desired goal is on its way to becoming a realized experience.

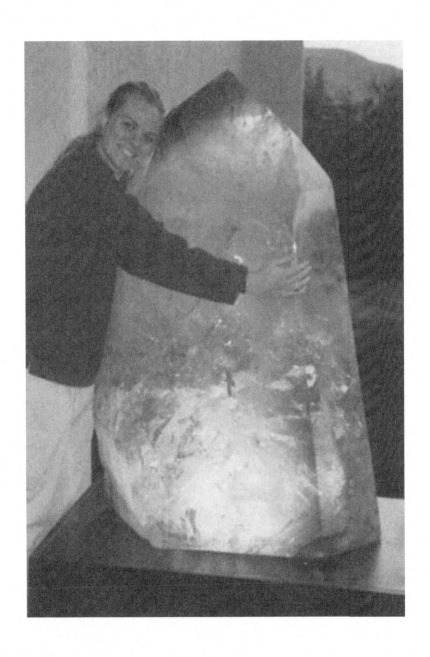

AFTERWARD

There is a higher calling that your soul is always asking you to step into. Although we can learn many different and wonderful things from books and other external resources, we learn mostly through experience. Wherever you are at currently in your life and no matter where it is that you intend to go, you can choose right now to step into your power and stand in your own light......the light of your awareness. Awaken to it, apply it, learn from it, benefit from it, and master it. Everything becomes possible when you are aware of what you are thinking and how you are feeling in every moment.

Awakening to higher states of conscious awareness allows you to see through the false illusions of the ego and into the true authentic you. Be empowered in the magnificent journey that is your life. Actively transforming your consciousness will not only bring you greater fulfillment and deep inner peace, it will serve the whole of human evolution on our planet.

The divine essence dances in my heart...where its presence is always felt and forever remains unseen!

ABOUT THE AUTHOR

Positive Thought Leader and author Elizabeth Diamond was born in Buffalo, New York. In 1996 she received a B.A in Communications at Canisius College after which she immediately moved to San Francisco, CA. In 1998 she enrolled into a hypnotherapy certification program and became a Certified Hypnotherapist. She spent the next few years deepening her knowledge base as a Reiki Master Teacher, Crystal Healer and Certified HypnoBirthing Practitioner. These achievements marked the start of a lifelong journey of personal transformation and realizing the self.

She is best known for her revolutionary technique, The Intentional Scrapbooking Method™, which demonstrates how to initiate transformation from the inside out using art as a tool to consciously create and attract successful desired outcomes. A passionate public speaker, Elizabeth shares her message through media and interactive coaching programs. As an artist, healer, teacher, and published writer, Elizabeth is passionate about raising awareness that awakening to higher states of consciousness can assist planetary evolution. Elizabeth currently resides in Western New York with her four daughters where she is writing her next book.

ADDITIONAL TOOLS FOR MASTERING SELF-AWARENESS

Visit www.masterselfawareness.com TODAY To Claim These Additional Self-Empowerment Tools!

Audio Mp3 Guided Meditation *"Awakening Self-Awareness"* –
Get ready to deeply relax as you tune into your natural state of being. This 30 minute guided relaxation takes you on a journey through a rainbow of color as each one of the 7 Mindsets is explored. This meditation is intended to awaken your awareness to the knowing of who you really are. Download this mp3 today!

FREE Color Reference Chart –
Our *7 Mindsets to Master Self-Awareness Reference Chart* condenses the content found within this book into one easy to read chart for quick reference. This colorful downloadable pdf serves to remind you where each one of the 7 Mindsets and its recommended crystal are located within the chakra system. Be sure to get this powerful tool today!

FREE 7 Week Teleseminar Series –
Our *7 Mindsets to Master Self-Awareness Teleseminar Series* further explores each one of the *7 Mindsets* outlined in this book for a total of seven consecutive weeks. These hour long seminars are intended to provide you with more insight and a deeper understanding as to how you can apply the *7 Mindsets* into your life. Learn more about the positive aspects of BEing that correlate to the chakra system, the recommended crystal, and

how to properly use the affirmations listed for each mindset. This is your opportunity to clarify any questions you have surrounding the content revealed within this book. Get ready to make quantum leaps toward your desired areas of personal growth. Take advantage of this offer today! Go to www.masterselfawareness.com to register for this once in a lifetime event!

BONUS: FREE Trial Offer to our Transformational Coaching Series
If you are serious about creating a life that reflects your heart's deepest longings than get ready to take advantage of this additional FREE offer! Join us for one of our transformational coaching calls from the series *"Get Out of Your Mind, Get Into Your Heart!"* To read more about this on-going program of support and community and to receive your FREE coupon code, please read more about it in the next section of this book called Recommended Resources.

RECOMMENDED RESOURCES

Creating Intentions **Transformational Coaching Series** offers an on-going opportunity to realize the full potential of your true creative nature, how to harness it, authentically express it, and joyfully live it through inspired action. All that is required is your willingness to show up to experience something new in your life.

Get Out of Your Mind, Get Into Your Heart!

The old way of living in fear, lack and struggle is over. We stand on the leading edge of experiencing life in an entirely new way. We do not have to learn lessons the hard way anymore. Learning through pain and suffering is a thing of the past. It is time for change. You hold within you the ability to transform self limiting behaviors and the capacity to reprogram old patterns of the past to excavate your divine essence and realize your deepest truths. All the resources you need to reclaim your power are already present and available within you. We offer the skills, the tools and the knowledge that will ultimately guide you back to you!

All change begins within and the truth of our inner nature is known when we are finally able to sit in the presence of it. For so long we have been approaching inner transformation through the level of the mind that is forever influenced by the ego. It is time to get out of the mind and into the heart, to create and experience lasting and sustainable change in every area of life. Engaging the energy of the heart is the focus of our series.

Be INSPIRED to:

- Awaken a powerful present awareness and focus
- Become grounded in loving compassion for yourself and others
- Differentiate between the false sense of self from the true you
- Become the observer and not the compulsive reactor
- Take action out of inspiration rather from fear or frantic worry
- Tune it to the inner wisdom and guidance of the heart
- Clear out stuck patterns and unwanted behaviors for good
- Put an end to negative thinking
- Raise set points for higher self-esteem and self worth
- Relax into the flow of your life rather than resist it
- Arouse deeper states of joy, love and deep inner peace
- Discover how to properly set intentions
- Work out the muscle of your imagination
- Embrace your unique inner strengths and talents
- Renew hope for what is possible in your life and then make it your reality
- Become a powerful magnetic force for the things in life you REALLY want
- Live your hearts highest calling
- Step into your complete, whole and fullest self
- Be authentic
- Live with integrity
- Become an active participant in the adventure that is your life!

We dedicate our purpose to the awakening of awareness within the mind, the heart and the soul. You are more powerful than you may currently realize. It is up to you to come to know just how incredibly unique and brilliant you really are. This is your true purpose in life.

Immerse yourself in possibility!
www.creatingintentions.com/membersite
Claim Your FREE Trial Offer TODAY!!!
Coupon Code: HEARTINTRO

THE INTENTIONAL SCRAPBOOKING METHOD™

Discover how easy it is to create and attract the life that you have always dreamed of using The Intentional Scrapbooking Method™. This DVD shows you how to MANIFEST what you really DESIRE and how to TRANSFORM self-limiting and self-defeating thoughts into more productive ways of thinking by harnessing powerful natural physical laws. Whatever it is that you desire, you will be EMPOWERED to design a life that you truly want to live after watching this DVD. Learn how the focused process of scrapbooking contains all the creative elements that SUCCESSFULLY imprint and re-pattern the subconscious mind to activate the LAW of ATTRACTION to produce the results you so strongly desire. One of the greatest satisfactions in life is to FULFILL a DREAM that you deliberately set out to create with your POWERFUL intent!

Live The Life You Have Always Dreamed About!

With The Intentional Scrapbooking Method™
YOU CAN EASILY and successfully **LEARN** how to:
- Become Clear of Your **PURPOSE** in Life
- Activate the **LAW OF ATTRACTION**
- Rewrite the **WAY YOU THINK**
- Deeply **IMPRINT** Your Subconscious Mind
- Cultivate Profound **JOY** and Inner **PEACE**
- Successfully Live Out All The **EXPERIENCES** of Your Deepest **GOALS AND DREAMS**
- **INCREASE** Your Capacity to **FEEL GOOD NOW!**

Upon awakening awareness to the nature of your true creative potential using the mindsets in this book, you are going to feel inspired to take action! Now is the time to channel the influx of positive energy that you feel by anchoring your new thoughts, ideas and intentions into concrete physical shape and form. Get ready to take your creative abilities to new heights!

The future of scrapbooking is scrapbooking to create the future!

Elizabeth Diamond demonstrates in this powerful DVD how to:
- Unleash the CREATIVE POWER of your thoughts
- Identify HIDDEN DESIRES
- CREATE a scrapbooking PROJECT from a SINGULAR INTENT
- LAUNCH YOUR DESIRES with a positively formed INTENTION
- Successfully JOURNAL your new story

Available Today!
www.creatingintentions.com

GUIDED RELAXATIONS & MEDITATIONS

If you are looking to relax into the peace and well-being that is already present at the core of your soul, Elizabeth Diamond offers a variety of guided meditations available in mp3 format to download and listen to at your convenience. This is a wonderful way to experience your natural state of being and at the same time harness your true creative potential. Just 10 minutes of focused relaxation will have you feeling more alert, alive, inspired, empowered, and filled with an increased amount of radiant energy. These meditations are an excellent way to nurture and replenish the self on a daily basis.

KEYNOTES, WORKSHOPS & SEMINAR PRESENTATIONS

7 Mindsets to Master Self-Awareness
Overview:

This powerful presentation will awaken your awareness to the positive mindsets that build a solid foundation for lasting states of inner peace, joy, and a deep love for life to exist in every arena. You already are everything that you have ever wanted to be. To realize your true inherent potential is to shift your awareness to embrace all the positive aspects that are currently present in your life. Change begins first on the inside. Nothing is more essential than your being able to feel the magnificence that is you! This program will open your eyes to how you can successfully harness your true creative power and how to infuse it into every single one of your actions from the ordinary to the extraordinary.

Topics Discussed:
- Activating the 7 Mindsets
- The Importance of honoring emotions
- Shifting to find the positive aspects and blessing in every experience
- Tuning into your natural state of being
- Identifying your starting point

Benefits:
- Cultivate a strong sense of trust and belief in the self
- Increase your ability to feel good
- Releasing old stuck thought and behavior patterns for good
- Living out your heart's deepest longings
- Awaken to a constant presence of intuitive knowing

This interactive presentation includes simple exercises that guide the audience to feel the peace and well-being that is available to them in every moment.

Other Keynote Topics Available:

Art is a Catalyst for Transformation and Change

Using Art to Create and Attract Future Outcomes

Living in Joy: Discovering Your Purpose and Heartfelt Mission

Birthing New Consciousness for Personal Growth and Evolutionary Development

Get Out of your Mind, Get Into Your Heart!

For Speaking and Media Inquiries

To book Elizabeth as a speaker at your event, please contact her manager, Jennifer Geronimo at JMGeronimo@aol.com

For more information on these and other programs, please visit

www.creatingintentions.com

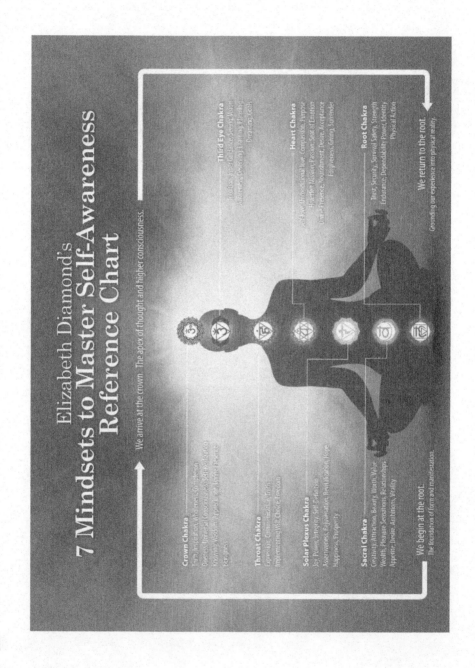

Elizabeth Diamond's
7 Mindsets to Master Self-Awareness
Reference Chart

We arrive at the crown. The apex of thought and higher consciousness.

Crown Chakra
Truth, Inspiration, Wholeness, Completion
Openness, Universal Consciousness, Self Realization
Knowing, Wisdom, Apple in our Infinite Presence
Release

Throat Chakra
Expression, Communication, Truth
Implementing Will, Choice, Freedom

Solar Plexus Chakra
Joy, Power, Integrity, Self Definition
Assertiveness, Rejuvenation, Revitalization, Hope
Happiness, Prosperity

Sacral Chakra
Creativity, Attraction, Beauty, Worth, Value
Wealth, Pleasure, Sensations, Relationships
Appetite, Desire, Ambitions, Vitality

Third Eye Chakra
Intuition, Inner Guidance, Seeing, Vision
Masterhood, Reasoning, Learning, Planning
Dreaming, Goals

Heart Chakra
Self Love, Unconditional Love, Compassion, Purpose
Heartfelt Mission, Passion, Seat of Emotion
Divine Presence, Nourishment, Desire, Acceptance
Forgiveness, Giving, Surrender

Root Chakra
Trust, Security, Survival Safety, Strength
Endurance, Dependability, Power, Identity
Physical Action

We return to the root.
Grounding our experience into physical reality.

We begin at the root.
The foundation of form and manifestation.

162

Chakras	Color	Location	Mindset	Crystal		Mission
Crown Chakra *Sahasrata*	Violet	Top of the Head	Be Present, BE Yourself!	Amethyst		Stills thought processes to open the gates to higher states of awareness.
Third Eye Chakra *Ajna*	Indigo	Between the Eyebrows	Seek Clarity!	Lapis Lazuli		Penetrates illusions of the mind & surfaces wisdom from the divine source.
Throat Chakra *Vishuddha*	Blue	Base of Throat	Laugh Often!	Chrysocolla		Assists clear communication of pure truth.
Heart Chakra *Anahata*	Dark Green/ Pink	Center of Chest	Love Yourself First!	Rose Quartz		Activates self-love, heals emotional wounds, & teaches unconditional love & compassion.
Solar Plexus Chakra *Manipura*	Yellow/ Light Green	Solar Plexus	Enjoy Yourself!	Peridot		Renews hope, strengthens personal power, & energizes the body.
Sacral Chakra *Svadhishthana*	Orange	Navel	Abundance Is Everywhere!	Carnelian		Assists recognition of the positive aspects & beauty found in every experience.
Root Chakra *Muladhara*	Red	Tailbone	Believe in Yourself!	Garnet		Ignites creative expression & assists physical manifestation.

163

CPSIA information can be obtained
at www.ICGtesting.com
Printed in the USA
BVOW03s2356271217
503832BV00001B/4/P